HOWARD THURMAN

The *Mystic* as *Prophet*

Luther E. Smith, Jr.

Friends United Press
Richmond, Indiana • www.fum.org

Friends United Meeting
101 Quaker Hill Drive
Richmond IN 47374
friendspress@fum.org
www.fum.org

Cover design by Shari Pickett Veach
Photos courtesy of Howard Thurman Family Archives and Arleigh Prelow, InSpirit Communications and Film.

Library of Congress Cataloging in Publication Data
Smith, Luther E.
Howard Thurman: The Mystic as Prophet.
Bibliography.
1. Thurman, Howard, 1900-1981. I. Title.
BX6495.T53S64   280'.4'0924   (B) 80-5961
ISBN-13: 978-0-944350-24-9

TO MY MOTHER AND FATHER
who reveal through love

Preface to Third Edition

Remembering is an essential religious practice for living faithfully in the present and into the future. When Howard Thurman died, I wondered if there would be sustained interest in his legacy. I knew that his witness and spirituality were worthy of extensive scholarship and reflection. I also knew that Thurman's speaking was often the inspiring occasion for becoming acquainted with his message. Would his writings alone continue to attract new generations to engage his ideas? Would the future benefit from his creative insights on personal identity, the reality of community, and the mystery of God? Would his initiatives in reconciliation be a resource for our increasingly pluralistic societies? These questions and more haunted me. Would Howard Thurman be remembered?

The years since his death have reassured me that Thurman's legacy continues to inspire and transform. Scholars have written dissertations, articles, and books about his significance. Courses on his spirituality are taught in seminaries. Magazines have devoted whole issues to interpreting his life and writings. The Howard Thurman Papers Project is now the second largest papers project on an African-American (only the Martin Luther King, Jr. papers project is larger). Thurman's writings are part of one publisher's "Modern Spiritual Masters Series." And he continues to be quoted by writers and speakers—even posters appear with Howard Thurman quotes.

Much credit must be given to Friends United Press for making his books available over these years. Without such support, the current state of Thurman's legacy would have been difficult, if not impossible, to achieve. I am also grateful to Trish Edwards-Konic, Editor of Friends United Press, for making possible the third edition of this book—its twenty-fifth year of publication.

Luther E. Smith, Jr.
Atlanta, Georgia
December 2006

Preface to Revised (Second) Edition

When *Howard Thurman: The Mystic as Prophet* was first published, it was my hope that the book would help persons understand the central ideas that inspire Thurman's theology and prophetic witness. I also wanted the book to stimulate scholarship on Thurman's significance as a major religious figure. Over the past ten years, readers' comments and the use of this book by Thurman scholars have been affirming responses to these initial intentions.

Since 1981, my research and writing on Howard Thurman has expanded upon themes presented herein. Still, this book has remained the primary source for my thinking and rethinking about Thurman. I therefore offer this revised edition with even greater confidence about its enduring value for interpreting Thurman's thought.

This revised edition is basically the same text as the original publication. Some extraneous references have been eliminated and a clarifying statement or two have been added. Minor changes in the syntax of some sentences and the division of paragraphs have been made to facilitate reading. Knowing that some readers dislike extensive reference notes, because such a style tends to be oriented to scholars, I was tempted to reduce the number of references.

But over the years I have come to experience these notes as old friends. Some of these friends serve as sources that help me to verify where Thurman expressed an idea, and they indicate where I might look to explore further his thinking. Others are friends that function as dialogue partners who confirm and debate conclusions of the text. If one does not care to visit with these friends, they have the courtesy to not impose themselves upon the reader. They remain available for the reader who might welcome their company.

I am grateful to Rev. Helen Pearson who gave helpful comments on the revised text, and to Ms. JoAnn Stone who assisted in the reading of galley proofs. Finally, I wish to express my appreciation to Friends United Press, and especially Ardith Talbot (Editor), for their interest in and professional commitment to publishing this book. Friends United Press, through its publication of Howard Thurman's books, has played a major role in sustaining Thurman's influence among scholars and spiritual pilgrims.

Luther E. Smith, Jr.
Atlanta, Georgia
December, 1991

(Editors Note: Following are the Preface and Acknowledgments to Smith's original work.)

Preface to First Edition

Study a prophet and you study his people. The prophet's significance is the result of his relationship with his community. His message, shaped by history and destiny, seeks to restore the community's sense of identity and purpose. The more we know about the prophet, the more we know about his people.

Howard Thurman's prophetic witness provides this kind of insight. His message evokes feelings and thoughts not only about his personality, but about the meaning of personal and social existence. In discovering more about Howard Thurman, we should know more about ourselves.

This book focuses on the thought of Thurman. Prophets prophesy. If we are to understand their sources of authority and explain their power in our lives, serious attention must be given to the content of their message. This study of Thurman primarily utilizes biographical data as it relates to his thought. The reader who is not acquainted with Thurman's life can find sufficient biographical information in his autobiography *With Head and Heart*. The "Bibliography" of Thurman's writings is included to aid those readers interested in further exposure to his work. I hope the following pages serve in helping us to understand and appreciate how prophetic presence enables our becoming a prophetic community.

Luther E. Smith, Jr.
Atlanta, Georgia
July, 1981

Acknowledgments

I am indebted to many persons who contributed in transforming an interest into a book. Dr. Howard Thurman's encouragement and availability were invaluable. In addition to extending full use of the Howard Thurman Educational Trust, he shared himself with an openness which not only provided me information, but insight. Ms. Joyce Sloan, Tape Librarian for the Trust, spent several days advising in the selection of recordings among the hundreds on file; her expertise was a major contribution to the thoroughness of the research. And Rev. Marvin Chandler, Executive Director of the Trust, has been most helpful in providing important materials since Dr. Thurman's death.

This book is a development of my dissertation, "An American Prophet: A Critical Study on the Thought of Howard Thurman." Dr. Allen O. Miller (chairman), Sr. Elizabeth Kolmer, and Dr. Thomas R. Knipp were the dissertation committee; their advising and support added to the depth of the inquiry. Bishop James L. Cummings, Ms. Elaine R. Smith, and the now late Mrs. Blanche Pitcher expressed many kindnesses, during the writing of the dissertation, for which I am deeply grateful.

Fr. Wm. James Walker suggested numerous bibliographical sources that aided my reading in Christian spirituality. Dr. Donald G. Shockley became the book's refiner's fire. His sensitivity to the material and written word sharpened the discussion. Rev. Rebecca Smith, Mrs. Helen Patton, Mrs. June Robertson, and Mrs. Dee Douglas were very helpful in the preparation of the typescript. And special appreciation goes to my wife, Beth, who has been a companion throughout every step of this journey.

Grateful acknowledgement is made to The Howard Thurman Educational Trust for permission to use extensive quotes from selected writings of Dr. Thurman; and to Harper & Row for permission to quote from Kenneth Cauthen's *The Impact of American Religious Liberalism*.

Contents

Howard Thurman
1900–1981

Chapter I

THE PROPHETIC CONTEXT

"Holy Man," "saint," "spiritual innovator," "one of America's greatest preachers and religionists," "prophet," and "spiritual mentor" are but a few of the titles and labels used to characterize Howard Thurman. Thurman (1900-1981) is one of the most popular American religious figures of the twentieth century. Across the country the name Howard Thurman evokes intense admiration and memories of inspiration.

To some people he illumines the peace and joy of the mystic way; to others he answers the most pressing problems of personal identity. There are persons who feel he clarifies the underlying spiritual issues of interpersonal relations; others stress his exposition of the religious dimensions of black Americans' struggle for justice and equality. And some primarily note his ministry of establishing models of inter-faith, inter-racial, and inter-cultural fellowship. These particular impressions, when pieced together, describe a life which has labored creatively to build the loving community.

Though Howard Thurman was not interested in forming a social action organization that embodied his ideas, or in becoming the leader of a mass movement, he has drawn a following which attests to the significance of his witness. Thurman devotees speak of his radical effect upon their lives, his gift for enabling peak experiences, guiding one to the presence of God, and sharpening the vision of reality. An *Ebony* magazine article describes the scope of his influence:

> Every year, scores of pilgrims—ministers, professors, students, workers, housewives, and government officials—make their way to the San Francisco headquarters of The Howard Thurman Educational Trust Foundation for spiritual guidance and counselling. Every week Trust officials send out scores of books, pamphlets, and cassettes bearing the fruits of 50 years of thinking and preaching. On almost any day of any week, large numbers of men and women gather singly or in groups at Howard Thurman Listening Rooms in America, Africa, Asia and Europe to listen to his words of meditation and challenge and solace.[1]

While Thurman has this ardent following, a large number of persons have never heard of him. This anonymity is, to a great extent, due to the failure of scholars to recognize Thurman as a significant religious thinker. Though a footnote reference is found here and there, and a few conscientious writers have written several pages on his ideas, there remains a pitiful dearth of scholarship on his thought.

An important function of scholars is to identify and assess the persons, ideas, and forces that shape society. Their printed word interprets who and what is worth knowing and worth passing on for the next generations to understand. Persons and events which are ignored by scholarship depend upon oral history and organization to keep their significance alive. These methods (oral history and organization) often fail to reach those of the populace who receive their education primarily through academies of higher education.

The lack of critical consideration of Howard Thurman can be ascribed to four causes: 1) Some religion and history scholars have never been exposed to Thurman. Their academic preparation and interest never dealt with his thinking and influence. Their lack of familiarity with black culture may explain the failure to consider his contributions. 2) Some scholars who are aware of Thurman's career dismiss his thinking as a repetition of pietistic themes, contributing no original ideas to America's religious life and thought. I have confronted several scholars who hold to such a position, and almost without exception discovered that they had not rigorously studied Thurman but came to conclusions after a cursory examination. 3) Consciously or unconsciously some scholars are intellectual racists; they cannot accept the fact that black people have made or could make a creative contribution to religious thought. A person like Thurman, therefore, never warrants their attention. And 4) Thurman's oratorical and personal power cause individuals to focus on the impact of his preaching and personality. A full length biography and numerous biographical articles primarily relate events in his life, present the inspiring motifs of his thought, and describe his charisma. There is little attempt to do an in-depth critical analysis of his ideas.[2]

The difficulty in overcoming the effect of personality, such that one is unable to appreciate the intellectual contributions, is brought out in an article about Martin Luther King, Jr.:

> King was regarded as a civil rights leader and as a man of extraordinary personal valor, but he has not been understood as a brilliant and mature theologian: the first two would, however, have been impossible without the third. It would be a tragedy, I believe, if we were to remember him only as a hero and not as thinker— by still giving our minds over to the authors of ponderous tomes and the orators on prestigious lecture platforms while giving over only our hearts to him. He deserves our head as well as our heart.[3]

Howard Thurman also deserves our head as well as our heart.

Profile of a Career

Born in Daytona, Florida, Thurman stayed in that city until the absence of educational opportunities for Negroes forced him to go to Jacksonville, Florida, for a high school education. He completed undergraduate studies at Morehouse College in Atlanta, Georgia, and his graduate studies in Theology at Rochester Divinity School in Rochester, New York.

When Howard Thurman graduated from seminary in 1926, he accepted the pastorate of the Mount Zion Baptist Church in Oberlin, Ohio. Thurman gives two primary reasons for taking this position: 1) the location of the church in a college town offered significant advantages for his personal development; with Oberlin College and its theological program he had the opportunity for graduate study and other educational resources (i.e., lectures, library, special work with Bible professors) which would continue to challenge and feed his mind; and 2) his temperament fitted the expectations for ministry of this college town church; he would not have to whoop, holler, or resort to any other such preaching styles in order to reach his congregation.[4]

In a short time the racial composition of the congregation began to change. White and foreign students from the college,

5

professors, and residents of Oberlin began to frequent his services, making this an integrated fellowship. He notes, however, "that during that entire period not a single white person ever joined the church."[5]

The mix of educational levels, ethnic and racial backgrounds, forced Thurman to "discover spiritual insights that moved at a profounder level than the contexts by which these insights were defined."[6] He realized that worship needed to address the common concerns of people from varied racial, cultural, and social backgrounds. Even in this first vocational post he was sensitive to articulating religion so that persons felt part of an inclusive experience. In Oberlin he began to experiment with worship as the context for realizing community.

The illness of his wife, which required moving to a milder climate, and his enthusiasm to work with students in an academic setting resulted in Thurman accepting a position in 1929 as Director of Religious Life and Professor of Religion for both Morehouse and Spelman Colleges in Atlanta, Georgia. After several months of independent study with the Quaker mystic, Rufus Jones, he began teaching in the fall of 1929. Here at two noted black institutions of higher education, Thurman enjoyed the intellectual stimulation which students provided. He also welcomed the opportunity to interpret religion and help shape the religious thinking of these young minds which were hungry for a spiritual

6

foundation for their lives.[7]

During his second year of teaching, his wife (Katie Kelly Thurman) died. In 1932 he married Sue Bailey. In this same year he received an invitation to join the faculty at Howard University in Washington, D.C. With more black Ph.D.s than any other educational institution, Mordecai Johnson, then President of Howard University, "had a dream of making Howard a place where the best [academic] minds and most able young black minds could come together and create, on behalf of the larger community, a whole new way to live in American society."[8] Johnson wanted Thurman to develop a religious life and program at Howard which matched the excellence of the school's other academic emphases. Thurman accepted this challenge and became Dean of Rankin Chapel and Professor of Christian Theology.[9]

During his tenure at Howard University, Thurman and his wife were asked to be members of a delegation on a "Pilgrimage of Friendship" to India, Ceylon, and Burma. The invitation came from the Student Christian Movement of these countries. In addition to his contribution as a creative religious thinker, Thurman's participation was considered important because "in a country divided by religious beliefs into Touchables and Untouchables, rich and poor, the testimony of representatives from another country's minority group might be far-reaching."[10]

Thurman and the delegation lectured and

7

discussed issues in forty-five academic centers in these three countries from October 1935 through the spring of 1936. He was questioned continually about the compatibility of Christianity with black people's struggle for human dignity. White Christians and churches had a history of being insensitive to black people's worth and freedom. Thurman answered these queries by distinguishing Christianity from the religion of Jesus. Despite this clarification, Thurman admits that:

> All answers had to be defensive because there was not a *single instance* known to me in which a local church had a completely integrated membership. The color bar was honored in the practice of the Christian religion. From a 10,000-mile perspective, this monumental betrayal of the Christian ethic loomed large and forbidding.[11]

It is out of this background that he had a religious experience at Kyber Pass (between Afghanistan and West Pakistan) which excited a vision that would determine the thrust of his social witness for the rest of his life. Thurman writes:

> We [Thurman and his wife] saw clearly what we must do somehow when we returned to America. We knew that we must test whether a religious fellowship could be developed in America that was capable of cutting across all racial barriers, with a carryover into

8

the common life, a fellowship that would alter the behavior patterns of those involved. It became imperative now to find out if experiences of spiritual unity among people could be more compelling than the experiences which divide them.[12]

Upon returning to Howard University he began to experiment with the arts, meditation, and innovative liturgies to create a worship experience which affirmed the unity within an audience which had religious, social, and philosophical diversity. These creative services were to evoke religious feelings that magnified the essence of religion, as opposed to religious dogmas and creeds that emphasized divisive differences. Members of the audience were not perceived as objects for theological discourse, but as subjects of experience. Thurman labored to test and prove the possibility for religion to establish community. He believed that the life of the spirit among different people had essentially the same needs. A common religious experience had the potential to transcend and diminish the meaning of all that separates.

These services were fulfilling to Thurman's convictions on the possibility for experiences of unity to override conditions and beliefs that divide. They did not, however, test the larger challenge which could only occur outside an environment like Howard University. The University was predominantly black and controlled (a student culture with similar goals, rules, habits, opportunities and restrictions; characteristics which did not reflect the patterns in the larger society).

When the invitation came to Thurman to help organize an inter-racial church in San Francisco, he saw this as an opportunity to realize his Kyber Pass vision.[13] San Francisco, with its cultural diversity, was not a controlled environment and could serve as a true laboratory for Thurman's dream. This was an opportunity to test the power of Christianity to overcome the separateness of discrimination, prejudice, and segregation— to test the ability of the Church to be a loving inter-racial fellowship—to test, as Thurman states, "the future of democracy."[14]

In 1944, Howard Thurman joined the Rev. Alfred G. Fisk in founding The Church for the Fellowship of All Peoples. It was the first church in American life which was inter-racial in its membership and leadership. Black and white people participated as equals in developing a Christian church. After Alfred Fisk's resignation from the church, Thurman assumed the ministerial leadership for Fellowship Church (this became the abbreviated name of the church).[15] The church continued to grow in membership and maintained its integrated character.

Thurman notes that until his departure from Fellowship Church in 1953, 60 percent of the membership was Caucasion, 35 percent Negro, and 5 percent other ethnic groups such as Mexican-American and Asian-

American. There was also a broad range of educational levels within the congregation.[16] In his book, *Footprints of A Dream*, Thurman describes the organizing, programming, worship, and fellowship of the church. He states that Fellowship Church's significance was not just in its ability to bring together separated groups, but in the quality of religious experience and life-changing effect which that experience provided individuals. The church created, through its worship and fellowship, opportunities for persons to have a proper sense of self and the urge to establish community.

His ecclesiology for social change was not to organize Fellowship Church as the base or spearhead for a mass social movement. Instead, Thurman placed importance on empowering the individual to live responsibly in whatever situations he or she works, socializes, recreates, or serves. Indicating the possible effectiveness of this method he says, "on almost every board of civic organizations in the city of San Francisco, including some labor unions, the membership of Fellowship Church was represented."[17]

Many were the difficulties and pressures in establishing this kind of church. But Thurman was a rebel with a cause. He concluded that the acceptance and existence of racially segregated churches was an anathema to the Christian witness. And his years at Fellowship Church reflected his genius and commitment in demonstrating the inclusive possibilities for Christian worship and fellowship.[16]

In 1953, Thurman received an invitation to become Dean of Marsh Chapel and Professor of Spiritual Resources and Disciplines at Boston University. He would be the first black person to hold such a crucial ministerial position at a major white university. He accepted the new position to: 1) test the viability of Fellowship Church as an institution which did not depend on his leadership, and 2) again be in a position to challenge young minds. This particular post, however, would test his religious insights and convictions among a predominantly white student population which also had many foreign students with varied cultural and religious backgrounds. On this campus of some 26,800 students, Thurman had primary responsibility for developing programs of religious nurture. Both university worship and the classroom would be laboratories for proving the urge of the spirit toward unity.

Since his seminary days, Thurman had been popular as a speaker at Y.M.C.A. conferences, religious retreats, and on college campuses. Young students were enthralled by his dramatic oratory and religious insights, and Thurman enjoyed the interplay with young minds which were open, searching, and critical. A ministry in institutions of higher education provided the appropriate context for stimulating his mind

12

to meet the challenges offered by educated youth. He constantly sought ways to speak the word and provide the experiences which made manifest the power of religion as a resource for creative personal and social living. One indication of his popularity among college youth is evident in the number of appearances he made as a lecturer. He spoke at over five hundred institutions internationally, with over four hundred of these same institutions being in the United States and Canada.

His influence was not limited to the campus. He often spoke to standing room only crowds at churches and civic auditoriums. From 1951 through 1954 he gave meditations on a San Francisco radio station which reached all of northern California. And from 1958 through May 1965 he gave weekly religious meditations on a Boston television station which reached all of New England. In calculating the extent of his influence, his career as a writer must be considered. He is the author of twenty-two books and over forty-five articles. This has distinguished him as the most prolific black writer on religion.

In 1965, Thurman retired from Boston University and gave his energies to the establishment and operation of The Howard Thurman Educational Trust. He devoted his life to its development until his death in 1981. The Trust's program has been to: 1) provide financial assistance to college students (particularly at black colleges) who have academic potential and financial need, 2) support programs and institutions which encourage inter-cultural understanding, 3) organize, code, duplicate, collect, and distribute Thurman's writings, taped meditations, sermons, and lectures, and 4) conduct seminars where persons from various disciplines have the opportunity to dialogue with Thurman on the significance of the life of the spirit. Along with the Trust's service activities, there has been a major emphasis to preserve and further the ideas of Howard Thurman in order to keep his witness alive.

Thurman's accomplishments can be best understood when held against the backdrop of American life. His times were not only marked by two world wars, the depression, social and political upheaval, but by a racism which manifested its nefarious power through Jim Crowism, lynchings, riots, racial defamation, segregation, and discrimination. Black resistance to these maladies ranged from Marcus Garvey's back-to-Africa campaign, to calls for a completely integrated society. This resistance sought to assure survival, affirm the integrity and dignity of black people, and establish an environment of justice and opportunity. This backdrop is Thurman's context. This is the context of prophetic formation and expression. This is the context by which the prophet is understood and assessed.

Defining   the   Prophetic

Thurman's primary identity was that of mystic. He was a mystic who recognized the necessity of social activism for enabling and responding to religious experience. This is evident when he says:

> Therefore, the mystic's concern with the imperative of social action is not merely to improve the condition of society. It is not merely to feed the hungry, not merely to relieve human suffering and human misery. If this were all, in and of itself, it would be important surely. But this is not all. The basic consideration has to do with the removal of all that prevents God from coming to himself in the life of the individual. Whatever there is that blocks this, calls for action.[19]

Religious experience (the encounter with God) is the purpose toward which life is directed. The experience gives identity, meaning, and perspicacity. But the possibility of religious experience is threatened when conditions in the social order prevent the God encounter.

Thurman's intense belief in the personal, private experience has resulted in his being labeled an advocate of personal piety. This labeling is not completely accurate. Although his insistence on self-awareness and transformation can be cast within the pietistic tradition, Thurman had just as intense a commitment to community. His mystical experiences were the basis for this commitment. He writes:

> It is in the moment of [mystical] vision there is a sense of community—a unity not only with God but a unity with all of life, particularly with human life. It is in the moment of vision that the mystic discovers that (his) "private values are undergirded and determined by a structure which far transcends the limits of one's individual self.". . .The ascetic impulse having as its purpose individual purification and living brings the realistic mystic face to face with the society in which he functions as a person. He discovers that he is a person and a personality [which] in a profound sense can only be achieved in a milieu of human relations. Personality is something more than mere individuality—it is a fulfillment of the logic of individuality in community.[20]

Society is not evil; it is not necessarily a barrier to creative living. Society contains much that is nurturing for the individual and the making of community.

The ability to determine critically society's good and evil, its prohibitive and instrumental dimensions, requires a retreat from society but not permanent isolation from and animosity toward it. Neither is the only way to transform society, as many pietists would claim, through the transformation of individuals. This kind of individualism was rejected by Thurman. Though acknowledging that transformed individuals are the first

16

step in remaking the social order, true community can only be established when transformed individuals act upon social structures and become involved in social mechanisms. Social action (demonstrations, running for public office, providing social criticism, community organizing, boycotts) is a natural consequence of personal piety.

In Segundo Galilea's article "Liberation as an Encounter with Politics and Contemplation," there is confirmation for Thurman's convictions about the process of moving from the autonomy of the mystic to the unity of community. Galilea writes:

> Authentic Christian contemplation, passing through the desert, transforms contemplatives into prophets and heroes of commitment and militants into mystics. Christianity achieves the synthesis of the politician and the mystic, the militant and the contemplative, and abolishes the false antithesis between the religious-contemplative and the militantly committed. Authentic contemplation, through the encounter with the absolute of God, leads to the absolute of one's neighbor. [21]

Galilea then describes effective responses to contemplation which make a better world (community). One response is political activity which involves the contemplative in party politics. A second response, which describes Thurman's commitments and ministry, is what Galilea calls "the prophetic pastoral option." He characterizes the option

17

as follows:

> In it [the prophetic pastoral option]
> charity, the source of contemplation, is
> channelled into the effective *proclama-
> tion* of the message of Christ about
> the liberation of the poor and the
> "least." The message becomes a *critical
> consciousness*, and is capable of
> inspiring the deepest and most decisive
> liberating transformation. In this sense
> it has social and political conse-
> quences.[22] (Italics added)

Thurman carried out this prophetic pastoral
option. His "critical consciousness" disclosed
the interrelatedness and interdependence of
all life—and how meaning and purpose
could only be experienced when one was
committed to supporting the relatedness and
dependence. Caring for others, then, is not
rooted in maudlin concern or an onerous
sense of obligation, but in the awareness
that caring affirms God's will for creation.
And in affirming God's will, one discovers
spiritual peace, joy, and wholeness.

Since the terms "spirit," "spiritual," and
"spirituality" are used extensively throughout
this book, they require clarification. Spirit
is the "breath of God" in creation, providing
value and meaning to existence. Realizing
and expressing itself in the material world,
the work of the spirit is historical and
political. It is the source for definition of
the individual, and the individual in
relationship to the collective. As it discerns

self, it discerns God, and what it means to be a creature of God.

The term "spiritual" is used as an adjective, indicating that something is "of" or "related to" the spirit. For example, a spiritual concern is a concern which relates to the well-being of, or the interest of, the spirit. A spiritual discipline is something one does to discern and express the work of the spirit.

Spirituality is a way of life committed to understanding the nature and urgings of the spirit. Life organizes all its desires, energy, and resources so that they might be dominated by the spirit. Spirituality brings a harmony to living that is consistent with the peace and will of God.

Although Thurman's followers might question the term, it will prove more useful to speak of him as an American prophet. The adjective "American" is not used, however, to limit the significance of his insights. The prophet's identity is deeply rooted in the history, ideals, hopes, and mission of his culture. Prophets are products of their culture, speaking to specific traditions, problems, and purposes of their culture. Their warnings and urgings deal with particular crises of their particular age.

America is the land of Thurman's nurture and prophetic witness. Thurman proclaims that the mistreatment of the nation's disinherited and acceptance of the will to segregate are betrayals of American and Christian ideals. In the tradition of the

19

Hebrew prophets he calls America and Christianity to recall the sources of their identity: for America the *Declaration of Independence* and *Constitution,* for Christianity the inclusive love-ethic.

Prophetic witness is shaped, made, and enacted in particular contexts, but its influence transcends its space and time. The Hebrew prophets had a prophetic message which informs the commitments of twentieth century people all over the globe. Prophetic witness endures. Time will demonstrate the strength of Thurman's word as a message for all seasons. Prophetic witness has an impact beyond particular contexts, and Thurman's thought should prove relevant wherever humanity is involved with the meaning and formation of community.

Chapter II

INTELLECTUAL SOURCES:
THE PIVOTAL MENTORS

The study of a creative mind eventually raises the question of intellectual sources. Who are the mentors? What are the informing philosophies? What life events shape the thought? Questions such as these attempt to uncover the primary influences upon the mind. This examination of Howard Thurman's thought begins by focusing on those persons who were pivotal in the formation of his thinking.

Four persons stand out as having a crucial impact upon the foundation of Thurman's thought: George Cross, Henry B. Robins, Rufus Jones, and Nancy Ambrose, his (Thurman's) maternal grandmother.[1] This chapter proceeds to: 1) clarify their influence in the development and shaping of Thurman's mind, 2) discern whether these persons represent a particular tradition of religious thought, and 3) determine their distinctive contributions in the making of the man.

George Cross

George Cross, Professor of Systematic Theology at Rochester Theological Seminary, Rochester, New York, taught Howard Thurman during the last year and a half (1925-1926) of his seminary education. In stating Cross's significance, Thurman says:

> He had a greater influence on my mind than any other person who ever lived. Everything about me was alive when I came into his presence. He was all stimulus and I was all re- sponse.[2]

Thurman so felt the need for this mentor that he arranged to meet with Cross on Saturday mornings to raise questions about class material and other faith concerns. The classroom and office visits were the settings where Cross reached Thurman.

An outstanding characteristic of Dr. Cross which impressed Thurman was the way he challenged students to be appreciative and critical of doctrines and dogmas. On Saturday mornings Cross offered the same challenge to Thurman. Commenting upon these sessions, Thurman says:

> . . . [Cross] took my little orthodox- ies and reduced them to whited ash. . . . [Cross] was the man who challenged every concept that I ever had and patiently taught me.[3]

An examination of Cross's writings provides deeper insights into his theological method and content. His book, *What Is Christianity,* is an excellent example of the teaching method which impressed Thurman. Cross defined the purpose of the book as an effort "to assist the intelligent Christian laymen and the ministers of the gospel who have felt the need of revising their doctrinal inheritance to reach a more satisfactory interpretation of the Christian faith."[4] He then embarked on a critical discussion of apocalypticism, Catholicism, mysticism, Protestantism, rationalism, and evangelicalism. He described the particular religious expression, its historical significance and impact, its strengths and weaknesses, and its value toward a more complete understanding of the Christian faith. The conclusion of this investigation was that these faith interpretations, either singularly or collectively, were not comprehensive enough in their attempts to define Christianity.[5]

Cross was in pursuit of an element which he could identify as the *essence* of the Christian faith. It is the basic, unchanging, unifying truth which characterizes and genuinely manifests the faith. This essential truth may be found in Christian doctrines, dogmas, creeds, and theologies, but it is never fully described through them. This essential truth has the fundamental qualities common to all religions, yet it distinguishes Christianity from other religions.

The essence of Christianity is what Cross endeavored to define through his method for doing apologetics.[6] This essence he characterizes in the following ways:

1. It is "a quality of spiritual life," where one acknowledges that one's ultimate interests and commitments must be with spiritual concerns.

2. The personality of Jesus Christ is the basis for understanding the essence. In Jesus, the Christian finds the perfect life. And through spiritual fellowship with this perfect life, its teachings and the meaning of its example, the Christian finds the way to "the higher life."[7]

3. It has distinctive qualities which are similar to other religions. It takes the individual into a consciousness of and relation to God which brings fulfillment to the heart like no other religion. Other religions are "Christianity in its beginning or lower stages."[8]

4. It is the practice of the most perfect human fellowship, where the potentialities in every person are appreciated, developed, and made available to the needs of others.

5. It is "one and the same with true morality." Love and devotion to God mean love and devotion to the welfare of our fellow man and woman.

6. It has the power for moral redemption, such that it delivers humanity from the dominion of evil.

24

7. It creates the experience of perfect peace for the believer. In the midst of suffering, fear and anxieties, this essence gives confidence and power to withstand and overcome.[9]

The teleology of this Christian essence is to lead the individual and community toward salvation. In his book, *Christian Salvation*, Cross defines salvation this way:

> . . .to the modern Protestant it is the bringing of the man into such a fellowship with God as gives him a self-mastery and a self-devotion to the highest end of life. It is the entrance into an experience of conscious unity of life with one's fellowmen, a participation in the ministry of a universal good. It is to be endowed with that spirit of enterprise that enables him to turn the forces of the material world toward their true end, to make them angels of mercy sent forth to do service for the sake of them that shall inherit salvation.[10]

There must be, according to Cross, individual salvation before the community can be saved.

Christian salvation is ultimately the movement toward "perfect community." Cross does not go into detail regarding the concept "perfect community." The concept centers on the idea of a place and time when the personality is able to exercise its full potential and be in loving relationship with other individuals, such that their personalities may seek their potential. Cross concludes that salvation is Christian essence realized in the life of the individual and community.

But there is another major emphasis in Cross's writing which completes his theological process. For the essence to be realized, and thereby become a saving force to prevent dogma, creeds, and other theological systems from becoming barriers to participation in the faith essence, the Christian mind must establish a *creative* understanding of the faith. The term "creative" means there are no outside-the-person definitions for Christianity; there are no fixed standard tests for this religion. Christianity is a religion that continually reveals its new meanings for the world. A total comprehension of this faith always resides in the future. It is a religion in "the process of evolution."[11]

Cross argues that the key to discerning the creative flow is in the human personality. He therefore states, "the interest in personality is the highest interest in life."[12] The personality interprets and remakes the cosmos. It is through the discovery of the perfect personality (Jesus) that a person finds his or her own personality, and therefore the answer to salvation. The personality is where Christianity is discovered, defined, and actualized for the transformation of the individual and community.

Cross's theological stance falls within the tradition of evangelical liberalism as explicated by Kenneth Cauthen in his book, *The Impact of American Religious Liberalism.*[13] Cauthen defines the tradition thus:

> They [evangelical liberals] stood squarely within the Christian tradition and accepted as normative for their thinking what they understood to be the *essence* of historical Christianity. These men had a deep consciousness of their continuity with the main line of Christian orthodoxy and felt that they were preserving its *essential* features in terms which were suitable to the modern world. One of the evidences of the loyalty of the evangelical liberals to the historic faith is the place which they gave to Jesus. Through his person and work there is mediated to men both knowledge of God and saving power. He is the source and norm of the Christian's experience of God. In short, evangelical liberalism is Christocentric.[14] (Italics added)

This tradition stresses a personality-centered Christianity, reason and experience, witness to moral and social issues, theological personalism, and an evolutionary revelation of the faith.

Cross's theology clearly conforms to evangelical liberalism. With this theological understanding, Cross emboldened Howard Thurman to look to Howard Thurman for the answers to his (Thurman's) religious questions. He encouraged Thurman to trust and value the insights of his own personality, such that it serves as the interpreter of religion that provides new meanings and directions for the faith.[15] Thurman comments on the significance of this teaching in saying:

> For the first time now a creative mind was bearing down on my mind and making me discover dimensions of my own creativity that I didn't know existed until I began to come under his teaching influence.[16]
> I think perhaps more than anybody else, . . . he [Cross] helped me discover my mind.[17]

Cross's influence was neither limited to introducing and impressing Thurman with evangelical liberalism, nor to the way this theology was a tool for self-discovery and affirmation. Cross played a major role in counseling Thurman on how to use his new sense of resource and ability. Just before Thurman graduated from seminary, Cross said to him:

> I think, Howard Thurman, you have the ability and the gift to make a creative contribution to American religious thought. You are sensitive, and you are a Negro. No one could blame you if you did battle on the racial problem but, as your friend, I say to you that to do that would be a waste. This must be done but your gifts are in another dimension.

> No white man has the right to say
> this, for he does not know what it is
> to be a Negro, but all social ques-
> tions are temporary questions. They
> are a part of the total growth of the
> race to maturity. If a man's energy
> goes into social problems, when that
> is no longer relevant his work is
> done. You, Howard Thurman, should
> address yourself to the timeless
> hunger of the human spirit. Doing
> so, your greatest capacities will be
> released.[18]

This encounter evoked in Thurman a feeling which corresponded to his baptism: that he was privileged to be the recipient of some awesome commission and confirmation. Later, in this and other chapters, his advice will come under closer scrutiny. Suffice it here to say, Cross made a significant impression on Thurman's understanding of his vocation and identity. The focus on the "hunger of the spirit" informs every endeavor of Howard Thurman's life.

Henry B. Robins

Henry Burke Robins was Professor of Religious Education and The History and Philosophy of Religion and Missions at Rochester Theological Seminary. Though Thurman took his course on the Philosophy of Religion, Robins's chapel meditations made the greater impression upon him.[19] Robins's messages, and particularly his manner, cast such a spell on Thurman that he appeared to be "talking from another plane."

Thurman was not only impressed with the content of Robins's messages, but with the style which emanated from his personality. During my interviews with Thurman there was the feeling that he was affected by the personality of his mentors, as well as their ideas. The style of challenge in their teaching and speaking said something about the quality of their theology. Thurman used such terms as "kind," "warm," "patient," and "soft spoken" in describing the influence of these men on his life. Thurman recalled that "when he [Robins] took chapel, I would pace my breathing, because I didn't want my breathing to interfere with the flow of his impact on my mind."[20]

Thurman's comment on Robins's effect upon him is: "It was he [Robins] who first defined for me the scent that had been in my nostrils a long time; that the spiritual experience of the human race was essentially one single experience."[21] The statement elicits the sense of a parallel emphasis between Cross and Robins. Cross primarily deals with a *Christian essence* which is found in all expressions of the Christian faith. Robins is credited with identifying for Thurman the *religious essence* which is found in all expressions of religion. Cross's essence is the cohesion factor for Christian Apolegetics. Robins's essence is the cohesiveness in Comparative Religion. Cross helped Thurman understand his faith within

30

its many traditions. Robins enabled him to understand his faith in relation to other faith claims.[22]

After a thorough study of Robins's writings, one can accurately conclude that what Robins means by religious essence is the same as Cross's "Christian essence."[23] Christianity's essence *is* religious essence at its most complete stage of development. Christianity does not do violence to the traditions of other religions. According to Cross and Robins, it helps them to see their tradition as an important stage in the evolution of religious consciousness, with Christianity as the culmination of the evolutionary process. Christianity, at its core, is universal in character. It has the ability to include and speak meaningfully to the religious aspirations of all the world's peoples. This universal quality makes it the greatest missionary religion.[24]

The parallelism between these two teachers continues throughout their theological development. The purpose of the essence for Cross is the "saved community." Robins uses a different term, "the Kingdom of God," to express the same concept. The Kingdom of God is the perfect human fellowship where redemptive love is fulfilled.[25]

Robins professes a method like Cross's "creative Christianity" that affirms the personality as the definer of the faith. Personality interprets reality and God's activity in it. The personality can discern how humanity's involvements work toward

31

good or evil. Experiences of living become the primary material for developing ethical principles and faith convictions. Personality keeps a faith responsive and relevant, and therefore alive to a world in the process of evolution.[26]

This outline of Henry Robins's theology indicates that he was also rooted in the tradition of evangelical liberalism. His thought reinforced George Cross's thought and the impact of this theological persuasion on Howard Thurman. These two men, whose personalities and ideas spoke most profoundly to Thurman, were feeding him the same intellectual diet. The terms changed but the basic concepts were identical.

As Cross was the one who commissioned Howard Thurman to garner all his energies to address the "hunger of the spirit," Thurman credits Robins as the teacher who "was as close to introducing me [Thurman] to the life of the spirit as any professor I had".[27] Cross raised the importance of spiritual matters. Robins gave definition to them, particularly their unifying and universal qualities. But most important of all, Robins led Thurman to an understanding of how he (Thurman) was to participate in the "spiritual adventure." Spirituality, said Robins, is not just an idea but an *experience*. Thurman received from Robins a deeper insight into the meaning of experiencing the life of the spirit.

In reflecting on Robins's messages,

Thurman recalled that only once or twice did Robins refer to mysticism, but Thurman came to believe that Robins was in fact a mystic.[26] Robins was a practitioner of that tradition which is at the center of Thurman's religious identity: mysticism. Mysticism was made manifest to him through the person of Henry Robins. Maturity in this interest, however, came through the careful tutoring of Rufus Jones.

Rufus Jones

Howard Thurman became aware of Rufus Jones through his book, *Finding the Trail of Life*. Upon finishing the book, Thurman had a feeling of "instant kinship" with the author. He initiated correspondence with Jones, and for six months during 1929 became a "special student of Philosophy" in residence with this Quaker mystic at Haverford College.

Rufus Jones gave Thurman his first extensive exposure to the historical, philosophical, and experiential dimensions of mysticism. Though Thurman had remembered experiences of mystical consciousness since childhood, this internship brought definition, discipline, and perspective to the experiences. Jones boldly underscored Robins's emphasis that religion be an experience. More than any other teacher, Jones formed the nexus that religious experience, at its profoundest level, is mystical experience.

33

Jones defines mysticism as:

> . . . *the type of religion which puts the emphasis on immediate awareness of relation with God, on direct and intimate consciousness of the Divine Presence. It is religion in its most acute, intense, and living stage.*[29]

And while he is ready to admit that mysticism is subject to critical review, it still is the surest "way to know God."[30]

Discovering one's true relatedness to God, Jones believes, is the most important commitment that can be made. Meaning and sustenance for all life come from this relatedness. This focus is what Jones calls "spiritual concerns" or "concerns for the life of the spirit." In the same vein as George Cross and Henry Robins, he considers this the ultimate interest of life, its *elan vital.*[31]

Cross's principles of Christian essence are reiterated by Jones. There is virtually no departure between the three teachers on their understanding of the identity of Christian faith. The essence of Christian mysticism is identical with Cross's "Christian essence" and Robins's "religious essence."[32] Distinctive to Jones is his emphasis upon mystical consciousness as the way to discern God's presence and will. This mystical consciousness reveals the Divine which requires a fellowship of mutual caring and serving, and a Divine which dwells in humanity. This consciousness is the basis for social transformation.

Jones is deeply committed to a theology which claims issues of justice, freedom, and peace as inherent interests of the religious venture.[33] Commitment to the spiritual life is a commitment to that power which is able to save the world. Spiritual issues are the very ground of all material issues (e.g., politics, civil rights, poverty, crime).

Jones not only disclosed for Thurman the necessary and renewing aspects of mysticism in religion, but he linked these aspects to world conditions. More specifically, he offered a linkage which *gave Thurman the vision of how spiritual power could address the conditions that oppressed him as a black man in America.* Howard Thurman confirms the significance of this link when he says:

> . . . all my life I have been seeking to validate, beyond all ambivalences and frustrations, the integrity of the inner life. . . . I have sought a way of life that could come under the influence of, and be informed by, the fruits of the inner life. The cruel vicissitudes of the social situation in which I have been forced to live in American society have made it vital for me to seek resources, or a resource, to which I could have access as I sought means for sustaining the personal enterprise of my life beyond all the ravages inflicted upon it by the brutalities of the social order.[34]

Rufus Jones was the person who gave him this crucial perspective: "He [Jones] gave to me confidence in the insight that the religion of the inner life could deal with the empirical experience of man without retreating from the demands of such experience."[35] Jones revealed the power of religion to answer all of Thurman's existential predicaments.

Whatever social theology Thurman picked up from Cross and Robins was realized in a new way through Jones. The inner life's teleology is to bring the Kingdom of God into reality—to form a world community where personality has a free environment in which to seek its potential, and in which love gives harmony to relationships.[36]

Again as with Cross and Robins, the personality is the means through which faith is creatively defined and applied to life situations. Since in Jones's mind God is "resident presence cooperating vitally with us and in us here and now as an Emmanuel God," the individual becomes the bearer and revealer of the faith.[37] The inner life is the source of meaning, healing, and hope.

Theologically, Rufus Jones comes from the same tradition of evangelical liberalism as Cross and Robins. Kenneth Cauthen creates the category "mystical liberalism" to highlight Jones's contribution.[38] Evangelical liberalism (and in one case mystical liberalism) was the theology of Thurman's mentors. They challenged and inspired their student with ideas from this school of thought. As it

36

informed Thurman's instructors, it shaped his mind.

Jones's theology reinforced Cross's influence in helping Thurman to gain confidence in the abilities of his personality for doing theology. This theology underscored Cross's commission on the significance in working on the hunger of the spirit. Jones's thought was also consistent with Robins's theme concerning the spiritual adventure of the human race and the necessity of religious experience. But Jones's focus on mysticism was a distinctive contribution which became integral to Thurman's identity. Mysticism is religious experience at more intense levels than stressed by Cross and Robins. The "immediate awarenesss of relation to God" was now part of Thurman's understanding of religious essence.[39]

Jones's other contribution relates to the new meaning he gave to Cross's advice that Thurman not give his energies to the race question but to spiritual questions. Jones eliminated any duality that may have been interpreted from this counsel. The race question, according to Jones's theology, could be forcefully addressed through a ministry to the spirit. Or more specifically, the race question could be understood as a spiritual question. Jones helped Thurman's mind to grasp ways to be intensely involved in the spiritual *and* social reality—involved without becoming schizoid. Thurman's intellectual energies could now have a singular focus, for the essence of religion must address the social order. The spirit hungers in, and because of, its cultural context.

Nancy Ambrose

Rufus Jones, Henry Robins, and George Cross owe whatever impressions they made on Thurman to the tutelage of his maternal grandmother, Nancy Ambrose. She not only cultivated his life, but his mind. She had such a pervasive and total influence on Thurman that she is examined last to put in proper perspective the contributions of the other three intellectual sources.

When Howard Thurman was seven years old, his father died. Since Thurman's mother had to work long hours in order to support the family, his grandmother took primary responsibility for rearing him.[40]

Cross helped Thurman discover the creative dimensions of his mind, but Nancy Ambrose prepared the way by stressing the value of the mind. Thurman says:

> The other thing I got from her was an enormous respect for the magic there is in knowledge. That came from what she had observed as a slave child. Whenever her owner's wife saw her daughter trying to teach my grandmother the alphabet or one, two, three, she would chastise the child and send her to bed without supper. My grandmother said: "I saw there must be some magic in knowing how to read and write."[41]

38

The interest which Nancy Ambrose had in Thurman acquiring knowledge went far beyond reading and writing. She continually pushed him to achieve, to reach his potential, to acquire the "magic."

He was the first black youth in Daytona, Florida to receive an eighth grade certificate from the public schools. Despite financial hardships he went to Jacksonville, Florida to obtain a high school education. His grandmother made these decisions for Thurman. She did not allow him to accept the educational limitations placed on black youth in their community.[42]

Cross, Jones, and Robins define Christianity as basically a "quality of spiritual life." Robins states that religious experience informs this "inner life." Jones takes religious experience to a deeper level and identifies mystical consciousness as the primary informer. Thurman's grandmother, however, had already manifested through her person, the spiritual and experiential essence of the faith. Thurman says:

> I learned more, for instance, about the genius of the religion of Jesus from my grandmother than from all the men who taught me all. . . the Greek and all the rest of it. Because she moved inside the experience and lived out of that kind of center, . . .[43]

She experienced the "immediate awareness" emphasis of mysticism:

> She [grandmother] couldn't read her name if it was as big as this chapel. But she had stood inside of Jesus and looked out on the world through his eyes. And she knew by heart what I [Thurman] could never know.[44]

It is difficult to know whether, during his formative years, Thurman was aware of her religious consciousness. However, it can be said that whatever she communicated during these early years impressed Thurman's adult life as a profound, mystical spirituality.

Nancy Ambrose was the first to teach Thurman that spirituality sustains one in the midst of life's many predicaments. Though Jones later clarified the power of mysticism to support and nourish the individual, Thurman's grandmother was the living demonstration of the concept:

> . . . she [grandmother] was a strong, positive, self-contained human being. Her life was full of tragedies—hunger, cold, the death of some of her children. But she had built-in controls. Only once did I [Thurman] see a tear on her cheek. . . . I got a certain kind of strength from her.[45]

She witnessed to the power of her spirituality to meet one of the fundamental demands of life's hierarchy of needs: the need to survive.[46]

This survival function of religion is not just addressing the condition of the body, but the survival of the *identity*—that center of a person which gives definition to one's being. His grandmother interpreted religious sources within a context which addressed Thurman's identity needs more pointedly than his other three teachers. Her spirituality targeted an area to which Cross, Robins, and Jones gave little or no attention. Her "religious essence" was not just in dialogue with concern for the world but with the particular issue of what it means to be black in America.

Nancy Ambrose did not allow her grandson to read from the writings of the Apostle Paul because the ministers who came to the plantation when she was a child would preach from the text, "Slaves, be obedient to your masters." Their hermeneutical approach went against the freedom ethos which characterized her religion.[47] In contrast, she often told the story of the black preacher who had a different message for the slaves. In their gathering he would say: "You are not slaves, you are not niggers—you are God's children." As his grandmother finished her story with those lines, a kind of transformation took place in her: "she would unconsciously straighten up, head high and chest out, and a faraway look would come on her face."[48]

This communicated to Thurman the function, power, and necessity of religion to speak to his existential concerns. If an idea or theology is to have any validity, it must justly deal with his life situation. It must affirm his blackness. It must affirm his worth as one of "God's children." His grandmother's influence made this a basic hermeneutical principle of Thurman's mind.[49]

Nancy Ambrose's influence on Thurman can be identified in fundamental concepts of his thought. Her insistence that religion caringly speak to her condition as a black person in America, her biblical criticism which distrusted the writings of the Apostle Paul (Thurman's criticism of Paul as one lacking intense sensitivity to the plight of the oppressed is developed in his book, *Jesus and the Disinherited*),[50] her intuitive understanding of religion, her feeling of nurture from mystical passages of scripture,[51] her negative reaction to violence, and her willingness to challenge the church's authority were all important in shaping Thurman's theology.

Nancy Ambrose cultivated the mind which was later sown by Cross, Robins, and Jones. She gave Howard Thurman a sense of respect for intellect and an appreciation for the "more of life" it makes available. She was a living precursor for the ideas about "the life of the spirit," religious experience, and the sustaining power of one's faith. Her influence was not at odds with the evangelical liberalism tradition which came into Thurman's life, but in many ways she prepared the way.

Thurman's mentors gave him distinctive yet

reinforcing concepts for the development of his thought. Nancy Ambrose's influence began during his childhood. She consistently integrated religion with the family's existential situation. The worth of self (which includes racial identity) and the strength and wisdom from knowing God were evident in her very being.

George Cross and Henry Robins influenced Thurman during a critical period when his perception of social and moral reality was being radically transformed. It was during seminary that interpersonal relationships with white students caused Thurman to realize that white people were to be included in his ethical considerations. The pre-seminary attitude is explained:

> When I was a boy growing up in Florida, it never occurred to me, nor was I taught either at home or in church, to regard white persons as falling within the scope of the magnetic field of my morality. To all white persons, the category of exception applied. I did not regard them as involved in my religious reference. They were not read out of the human race—they simply did not belong to it in the first place. Behavior toward them was amoral. They were not hated particularly; they were not essentially despised; they were simply out of bounds.[52]

At a time when his ethical "field" was widening, so was his theology. Cross and Robins provided a theological framework

43

that supports an ethic of inclusivity. By defining essentials of faith they undermined dogma and doctrines that tend to alienate rather than unify religious people.

Rufus Jones magnified the interdependence of the spiritual quest and social change. The emphases of Ambrose, Cross, and Robins were blended together in Jones's mysticism to form a theology which undergirded Thurman's beliefs and commitments as he began his career.

These mentors lived and taught a spirituality that nurtured Thurman's mysticism. They (especially Ambrose and Jones) exposed the necessity for religion to address prophetically conditions of the social order. They helped shape the mystic and the prophet.

Chapter III

THE THEOLOGICAL FOUNDATION

The cover of *Common Ground: Essays in Honor of Howard Thurman* identifies Thurman as "Theologian, Professor, Minister, Lecturer, Author, Artist, [and] Founder."[1] "Theologian" is a major title which is often neglected in studies on Thurman. As a theologian he makes an invaluable contribution to the American religious scene. Teaching, writing, pastoring in churches and college chapels, lecturing and administrating are the media through which this central life's labor is accomplished.

Several scholars have recognized Thurman's contributions as a theologian. Ralph G. Turnbull, in his *A History of Preaching*, Volume 3, believes that Thurman's "creative mind has brought new standards to Black worship and theology."[2] Thurman is understood as a seminal theologian and not just a "great preacher." The significance of Thurman's intellect is asserted by Joseph R. Washington, Jr. in his book *Black Religion*. Washington calls Thurman "the most provocative innovator in the spiritual realm yet produced by the [Negro] folk," and he believes "Thurman has come as close as any Negro to being a theologian."[3] John D. Mangram, a Professor of Religion and Philosophy, considers Thurman as "the most articulate interpreter of the Christian understanding of existence among black American church persons," and that Thurman "has been 'Mr. Black Theologian' for quite awhile."[4]

Howard Thurman resisted being called a theologian. To him the term refers to one who attempts to define and describe God's nature, character, and action. Thurman felt that theology ignores: 1) the vitality of religion which refuses to conform to a system of definition and description, and 2) the significance of the theologian as religious subject.

Allen O. Miller, in his book, *Invitation to Theology: Resources for Christian Nurture and Discipline*, gives a definition of "theology" and "theologian" which includes the concerns for vitality and religious experience—a definition which eliminates the "religion" (spirit)—"theology" (intellect) dichotomy. He says;

> . . . Although theology means literally "a discourse about God," its content is more like a prayer of praise and thanksgiving than a scientific description of a matter of fact . . . the human response which the mystery of God evokes is primarily appreciation and commit-

intellectual satisfaction.

. . . Doctrinal beliefs are an important part of theology, but they are not the heart of it. The heart of theology is like the heart of religion and of morality, a personal relationship. Moreover, all three express action. In fact, in our Christian understanding, theology, religion, and morality are all concerned with activity—the activity of God's holy love in human affairs.[5]

This understanding of "theology" and "theologian" is being used in this discussion—an understanding which appropriately identifies Thurman as a theologian.

This chapter outlines Howard Thurman's theology. Neither Thurman nor his biographers has systematically organized his thought. Thurman was not concerned that his beliefs about God, Jesus, the Church, humanity, and nature be compiled in a systematic theology. He had a bias against such an approach for he felt that once the system is formed, it is not able to speak to life in all its fluid manifestations. Life is so dynamic that it requires religious insights which are as equally dynamic, equally prepared to change with the new demands or revelations which life brings.

A system, Thurman believed, inhibits the ability of religion to do this. With a systematic theology one is not open to the continual newness which comes from religious experience.[6] However, Howard

Thurman articulated in a consistent manner the tenets of his theology. Out of his writings and speeches, one can extract a core of ideas which constitute his theological foundation.[7]

The Vision of Community

Howard Thurman identified community as the single most important quest of his life. It had occupied his thoughts and activities since childhood.[8] Defining community is the end purpose of his theology. Establishing community was the commitment and labor of his ministry.

The basic principle behind Howard Thurman's concept of community is that "the literal fact of the underlying unity of life seems to be established beyond doubt." He develops this principle in saying:

> If life has been fashioned out of a fundamental unity and ground, and if it has developed within a structure, then it is not to be wondered at that the interest in and concern for wholeness should be part of the conscious intent of life, more basic than any particular conscious tendency toward fragmentation.
> . . . It [reconciliation] seeks to effect and further harmonious relations in a totally comprehensive climate.[9]

Thurman's book, *The Search for Common Ground,* is devoted to verifying this principle by examining the creation myths of cultures, the life sciences, the philosophy behind utopias, and the social psychology of change in America. Thurman believes that the urge for and toward community, toward harmonious unity in life, can be found everywhere from the smallest cell to the whole universe.

This principle is integral to the tradition of mysticism. Rudolf Otto, in this classic, *Mysticism East and West*, labels this principle as "the way of Unity." Whoever sees reality, according to this tradition, will find a relatedness in life which eliminates any perception of contradiction. This "unifying vision," says Otto:

> . . . results in the peculiar logic of mysticism, which discounts the two fundamental laws of natural logic: the law of Contradiction and the Excluded Third. As non-Euclidian geometry sets aside the axiom of parallels so mystical logic disregards these two axioms; and thence the 'coincidentia oppositiorum,' the 'identity of opposites,' and the 'dialectic conceptions' arise.[10]

In advocating unity, Thurman is not ignoring or denying forces of evil, destruction, and division. These forces exist, but they are not aligned with the ultimate intent of life. They are against life, and therefore will not be supported by it. Whatever divides and destroys cannot be nourished by that which unites and creates;

it can only feed on itself and ultimately consume its own existence. This leads Thurman to say, "the contradictions of life are not final."[11] That which is vital (in that it assures the continuance of the creative process), which brings together disparate experiences and components, is a truer manifestation of the movement and intent of life. Life is on the side of unity, and those motives and forces which enable unity.[12]

This unity, as it relates to Thurman's concept of community, is characterized by its ability to allow persons (and nature) to actualize their potential. In actualizing potential, persons come to recognize and realize their worth and purpose for life.

Also essential to community is reconciliation. Thurman considers the terms "reconciliation" and "love" to be synonyms.[13] He defines love as "the intelligent, kindly but stern expression of kinship of one individual for another, having as its purpose the maintenance and furtherance of life at its highest level."[14] Love responds to an individual's basic need of being cared for. It participates in the attempt to actualize potential, and therefore completes the fragmented and unfulfilled personality. But at a larger level, it brings together separated lives. It makes apparent the significance of relationships by stressing how inter-dependence is inherent in all of life. Love makes community.

Even nature is involved in this concept of community, for the love-ethic extends to plants, animals, and the rest of creation. His analysis of the cause for some cases of mental illness is an excellent example of this conviction of inter-dependence:

> Our atmosphere is polluted, our streams are poisoned, our hills are denuded, wild life is increasingly exterminated, while more and more man becomes an alien on the earth and a fouler of his own nest. The price that is being exacted for this is a deep sense of isolation, of being rootless and a vagabond. Often I have surmised that this condition is more responsible for what seems to be the phenomenal increase in mental and emotional disturbances in modern life than the pressures—economic, social, and political—that abound on every hand. The collective psyche shrieks with the agony that it feels as a part of the death cry of a pillaged nature.[15]

All life is related. Life is a unit. If community is to be established, love must be the prevailing ethos of relationships.[16]

The formation of community is the teleology of life. The vision of community gives value, structure, and purpose to life; it saves life from meaninglessness, frustration, despair, boredom, anxiety, and chaos. Community is salvation; it is life at its highest level.

Thurman believes that community can be realized in time and space. This vision is not relegated to another dimension (i.e., after death, in heaven, after a God initiated

51

apocalypse). This vision is an historical (in time and space) possibility. Love has the power to form community here and now.

The experience of community happens in two ways. One, the individual, through religious experience, can feel a kinship with all life. The individual, be it through meditation, service, scientific inquiry, or some other commitment to seeking truth, can become aware of the unity, the "Oneness" of life. This unity yields a personal, inward experience of community.[17]

The second way community is experienced is through the establishment of relationships which encourage and are sustained by love. This is Thurman's vision for the outward reality of community. The vision refers to the creation of community between individuals, in the family, within and between neighborhoods, within and between countries. Love transforms isolated and apathetic lives into related and caring ones.

These two experiences of community reflect its "now and yet to come" quality. While community is being experienced, one is also aware that greater boundaries must be sought. Experiences of community prove satisfying and dissatisfying at the same time. Community can therefore be a reality, and at the same moment be a reality to come. The world, through the efforts of those who are committed to love, must move toward the only destiny which can bring fulfillment to its creative spirit. It must move toward community!

Religion

Howard Thurman believes that religion is the conduit through which love creates this full community. He says:

> Somehow we must find that which is big enough to absolve us from artificial and ineffective methods for increasing welfare and well-being. This means the large view, the great faith, which will release the vast courage capable of sustaining us in the long pull toward a valid increase in welfare and well-being. It is for this reason that a religious faith about life and its meaning becomes a necessity for all who would work for a new heaven and a new earth, the achievement of which is literal fact.[18]

Further defining of Thurman's "religious faith," his theology, should reveal his ideas on how religion transforms human energy into community-making power and the human condition into community.

The Centrality of Personality

Thurman believes that community results from a sense of unity with life (inter- and intra-relatedness). This is only possible if the individual has a "sense of self" (inner-relatedness). *The development of Thurman's theology begins with the individual.* In his article, "What Can We Believe In?," Thurman's response to this question is "not only can I believe in myself, but I *must* believe in myself."[19] He believes that the individual personality is of infinite worth, and that its significance and nurture are essential concerns of religion. In understanding the principles which affirm, sustain, and give meaning to the individual, one has the key to understanding that which affirms, sustains, and gives meaning to the universe.

This emphasis on the centrality of personality to religion squarely puts Thurman in the company of Cross, Robins, and Jones. As stated previously, personality centered Christianity is a basic tenet of liberalism.[20] The romanticism of Friedrich Schleiermacher must also be credited with providing much of the intellectual rationale for this focus within liberalism. Schleiermacher's stress on the individual's self-consciousness (feeling) as the basis for religion has religion starting with the human situation.[21]

In Thurman's mind, two affirmations are important for a true sense of self. First, since a person's "fact" (one's inherent worth) is of ultimate value, it is important that one's self-image conform to one's self-fact. If an individual allows his/her worth to be determined by others, or by his/her own inadequate self-image, then one loses the freedom, guidance, and power which comes from the self. One forfeits one's life to another. In losing this control, a person's condition changes from freedom to slavery, and one's definition changes from human to tool. Thurman is convinced that an accurate sense of self is the only "basis that the dignity of man, the individual, can be restored."[22]

Secondly, though one's fact is inherent, the nurture of this fact toward a healthy self-image is a social function. Thurman says:

> We are all related either positively or negatively to some immediate social unit which provides the other-than-self reference which in turn undergirds the sense of self. Such a primary group confers *persona* upon the individual; it fashions and fortifies the character structure.[23]

Here again his thought accents the theme of unity and wholeness. Relatedness is a truer manifestation of reality than isolation or separateness. Inner-relatedness depends upon inter-relatedness, and inter-relatedness depends upon inner-relatedness. The self depends upon the community, and the community depends upon the self.

Just as the self and community are interdependent, they are also sustained by the same force of love. Thurman uses the term "self-love" to describe the necessity of love for the formation of the self. He writes:

> Self-love is the kind of activity having as its purpose the maintenance and furtherance of one's own life at its highest level. All love grows basi-

cally out of a qualitative self-regard
and is in essence the exercise of that
which is spiritual. If we accept the
basic proposition that all life is one,
arising out of a common center—
God, all expressions of love are acts
of God.[24]

Self-love in this short quotation takes on
considerable importance. The crucial insight
is that self-love, while affirming the
individual life, is also the source which
points the individual away from a
narcissistic self-centeredness. It is the source
for ethics and morality, it is the source for
wider expressions of love, it manifests the
spiritual life, and it witnesses to the
presence and activity of God in life. Self-
love is the experience which permits
inclusive living. It permits the individual to
move "from self to God."[25]

Freedom and Responsibility

Crucial to Thurman's understanding of love
is his conviction about human freedom. If
love is concerned with the "furtherance of
life at its highest level," it is thereby
continuously laboring to transform the present order of things. It is continuously laboring because the present order does not
represent life at its highest level. Thurman
says:

Always there seems to be something
more to be experienced, to be felt,

> to know. My mind rejects any conclu-
> sion as being final. The greatest
> source of hope, therefore, for both
> the present and future, is the aware-
> ness of potential in me, in other
> people, in life itself.[26]

Human freedom allows men and women to choose the most loving way to act in life. It gives them responsibility for determining the movement toward the higher life.

If one does not have any choice, then one does not have any responsibility. If one does not have responsibility, then love is not operative. If love is not operative, then community is impossible.

Love and freedom permit the individual to live the *committed* life which works for community. "Commitment" is a major theme in Thurman's theology. In his book, *Disciplines of the Spirit*, it is the first discipline considered; for without commitment, the other disciplines (growth, suffering, prayer, and love) are meaningless. Commitment orders, focuses, defines, and channels the use of life's resources. It also moves the individual from a false self-centeredness. It illumines the reality that "our life is not our own"— that life is lived in inter-dependence with our fellow men and women, inter-dependence with nature, and most important of all, inter-dependence with God. This awareness not only devotes life to an other than self concern, but in this devotion the self is given a greater sense of its own meaning.[27]

Human freedom, then, is essential to love's commitment toward community-making. Thurman feels that this freedom is not only essential, but it is always operative. A person never loses the opportunity, and therefore the responsibility, for creating community. A person keeps the initiative over the living of his or her life.

Thurman explains this assurance when he writes:

> For I believe that there is always something that can be done about anything. What can be done may not alter the situation, but the individual may relate to unalterable situations within the context of his own choosing. In other words, I am saying that a man need not ever be completely and utterly a victim of his circumstances despite the fact, to be repetitive, that he may not be able to change the circumstance. The clue is in the fact that a man can give his assent to his circumstances or he can withhold it, and there are a desert and a sea between the two.[28]

Lloyd J. Averill in his book, *American Theology in the Liberal Tradition*, classifies this liberal doctrine as the belief in the "free moral agency" of humanity. The moral possibility coexists with the moral imperative. Or as Averill says, liberals have the "confidence that 'I must' necessarily implies 'I can.'"[29]

This principle was very much a part of

romanticism. Paul Tillich describes romanticism as "a philosophy of imagination." Imagination empowers the individual to remain dynamic, vital, and moral within his/her environment. Tillich says: "The ego is creative, and everything in the world is only a limit to the ego; but the innermost nature of reality is freedom. . . . He who is not able to transcend the given situation in which he lives through his own imagination finds himself imprisoned in that situation."[30]

Freedom is crucial to Thurman's optimism about the possibility for community. It means that all which stands against community can be overcome. Something can be done to alter the most distressing situations.

An example of Thurman's convictions about the ability of human endeavor to achieve community is found in his meditation "A New Heaven and a New Earth." This phrase which comes from the *New Testament* book of *Revelation* (Chapter 21) is often used in the Christian Church to describe the eschatological time when God will judge humanity and establish God's Kingdom. All of creation will be made new and experience transformation under God's power. Thurman uses the phrase, however, to describe that which is possible if more persons give themselves to "increasing welfare and well-being."[31] The responsibility and opportunity rest with humankind. The eschatological, the radically new, comes through the person.

This belief in the power to create community can also be stated as Thurman's belief in the possibility for a perfect universe. He says that within all creation "there is a built-in sense of the possibility of experienced fulfillment and perfection."[32] *Goodness is the essential nature of humanity and all creation.* This goodness is trying to realize itself historically. This goodness, as in much of liberal theology, is identified as the *imago dei* (the image of God). God's immanence in the universe gives assurance that the creative impulse will be omnipresent and omnipotent. Since the contradictions of life are not final, and since God (as creative and loving power) is immanent and active in all things, the universe moves toward a destiny of community.

Thurman's insistence on freedom for establishing a new world order can be identified as a characteristic of the prophet. The prophet reveals how present realities neither reflect the will of God nor the potential of the people to effect change. Freedom, as described by Thurman, is the basis of hope. Hope enables humanity to anticipate and participate in bringing to fruition a future full of God's promise.

The Transformation of Evil

The destiny toward community is not automatic. Evil participates in reality and thwarts the realization of goodness. Thurman takes evil seriously. He does not consider it an illusion, but as a powerful force in the universe. He defines evil as "positive and destructive as over against that which is positive and creative. It manifests itself in forms of pain, suffering, and varying degrees of frustration."[33] Evil appears to be as "built-in" the nature of life as goodness.

Evil does not, however, have the last word. It is not ultimate. Even as evil is active in the lives of men and women, it becomes the ingredient for personal growth. It tests the moral fiber of the person, and by stretching and straining makes the fiber stronger. Crisis provides insight into one's weaknesses and strengths. It smashes any illusions of security or perfection. It initiates the person from innocence to maturity. It forces the personality, for the sake of survival, to discover and garner its spiritual resources. Evil can be instrumental in shaping community.[34]

This is not to cherish and celebrate the existence of evil as a necessary element for growth. This conceptualization does recognize, however, the creative capability of personality to grow in the midst of no-growth circumstances. The personality is able to find faith in the midst of fear, healing in the midst of suffering, love in the midst of hate, hope in the midst of despair, life in the midst of death, and community in the midst of chaos. The personality can experience community (salvation) even if the external circumstances do not support community. This is the personal, inward reality of community which was discussed earlier. It is, as Thurman quotes from Philippians 4:7, "The peace of God which passes all understanding."[35]

But the personality not only can discover its own salvation in these circumstances, it can remake the cosmos and create community for the world. There is power in the personality to triumph over evil, over all which stands against community. The power of love, which resides in the personality, is ultimate.

The Meaning of Jesus

Jesus of Nazareth, in Thurman's mind, is the revelation of how personality creates community; he personifies the transforming power of love. Unlike many mystics and romanticists, Thurman takes great interest in the historical Jesus.[36] The conditions and circumstances of Jesus' life are significant in understanding Christianity and the meaning of Jesus to the world.

Thurman highlights these "facts" of Jesus' life:[37] 1) He was a Jew; which meant he was part of a great religious and social heritage that worked at a covenant relationship with God. Being Jewish he also knew what it meant to be an oppressed minority. 2) He was poor; he did not have the privileges and advantages which wealth makes available. 3) Jesus was fully human; he struggled as all humans struggle with the difficulties of life. Jesus was not immune to hardship or failure. (I have not come across one Thurman reference to Jesus performing miracles. Jesus' life is also governed by the natural order. The "miracles" of Jesus are not in supernatural feats, but in the way he inspired persons to have an accurate sense of self and community.[38]) And 4) Jesus was fully divine; but there was no more God incarnate in Jesus than any other man or woman. Jesus had a greater consciousness of, and relationship to, his divinity. This consciousness was the result of Jesus working at a closer relatedness to God.[39]

The next concern of Thurman, which is a major characteristic of liberals, is to determine the essence of Christianity. This means distinguishing Christianity (the faith as interpreted by the Church) from the religion of Jesus. Thurman's *Jesus and the Disinherited* is aimed at discovering the genius of "Jesus as religious subject rather than religious object." He attempts to describe the religion of Jesus—a description which should yield Christianity's essence.[40] The religion of Jesus is characterized by the following concepts:

> 1. The individual personality has ultimate significance. The person is a "child of God," and this status has no superior. The welfare of each member of God's creation is important to the welfare of the whole creation. Containing the *imago dei*, the individual personality is able to express love

throughout creation and bring the universe to its proper state of harmony.[41]

2. The quality of the inner life is primary. An accurate sense of self is necessary if one is to transform the social order into a community. This accuracy is only possible if the individual is rooted in and committed to the spiritual life.[42]

3. God is concerned about the individual personality, and expresses this concern through a Fatherly love. Individuals are not tools to God's master plan for creation, but they are God's children. The individual is cared for by God in tender, personal, intimate, and parental ways.[43]

4. Respect for personality is the basis for love. This respect takes the focus away from the circumstances of a person's life (i.e., race, social status, religion, nationality) and puts it on his/her inherent worth. It recognizes the individual as God's child, and therefore, as one's brother or sister. This recognition puts all individuals within one's loving circle, within that "ethical field" where one feels responsible for the caring of others.[44]

5. Jesus placed all meaning and hope for life upon the love-ethic. Self-love, love between individuals, and love of God are the various manifestations of love which are the basis of community. Only love can shape, empower, and sustain community.[45]

6. Mystical consciousness was part of Jesus' life. It deepened his sense of self and his intimacy with God. Jesus' whole identity depended upon his mystical experiences. These experiences made him sure of God's presence, love, and commission for a ministry of love.[46]

7. God is the source of all life, meaning, and the realization of community. One can have complete confidence in God's love and power. God will not only remain close to the individual but will supply assurance for a fulfilled life.[47]

8. Community (salvation) is not a beyond this world hope but the possibility for God's love to triumph in history. Jesus' message of salvation is eschatological in the sense that it pronounces the ability to experience salvation here and now.[48]

With this conceptualization of the religion of Jesus, Thurman concludes that "Christianity as it was born in the mind of this Jewish teacher and thinker appears as a technique of survival for the oppressed."[49] Until this statement, Thurman's theology follows the traditional liberal viewpoint on the religion of Jesus. But now Thurman's racial concerns spark a truly creative analysis of the relationship of Jesus to the disinherited. This analysis will be discussed in greater detail in the next chapter. Suffice it here to recognize Thurman's insight as an outgrowth of his search for Christianity's

65

essence.

Thurman surmises that Jesus' religion was accepted by many as a survival technique because he gave them a vision of a great ideal: the love-ethic. This ideal challenged their lives to experience ultimate love, and therefore, a "peace which passes all understanding." A love and peace which gave them initiative over the living of their days. People believed in this religion because they believed in Jesus. In Jesus they could see the fullness of life which they wanted released in themselves. It is this influence of Jesus which reaches across the ages and continues to touch lives. As Thurman says, "the Christ of experience and the Jesus of history" are reconciled. Therefore, the life of Jesus has meaning for people today.

The meaning, the reconciliation, is explained by Thurman in the following way:

> The former [the Christ of experience] has to do with the creative synthesis of all the dreams and aspirations and longings of the human spirit for perfection of spirit, mind and character— the glowing triumph of spirit over matter, of purity over impurity, of holiness over sin. It is the revelation of the highest reaches of the quest for fulfillment. The latter [the Jesus of history] is earth-bound. It deals with a plodding goodness in the midst of ordinary difficulties. It points up the possibilities of direct human goodness in a society that operates upon the principle of selfishness, greed and lust. It lifts the hope of the moral

> and the ethical, in the midst of the
> immoral and the unethical. They need
> not be two different experiences;
> they may be a single aspect of one
> dynamic religious dedication.[50]

People today identify the spirit which informed Jesus' life as the same spirit which informs their lives. Jesus expresses the spirit in such a perfected form that inspiration and hope are given his followers.

In this way, the life of Jesus exercises a moral and spiritual influence over contemporary lives. Jesus reveals that fulfillment in life can only come by surrendering one's self to the will of God. Jesus is the revelation of how personality perfects itself and creates community. Jesus is the revelation of salvation.[51]

Jesus, in Thurman's theology, is not God, but he is "the for instance of the mind of God."[52] In knowing Jesus, one knows more about God. Thurman rejects the mysticism which focuses on Jesus as "reality itself" (as God). Thurman's mysticism views Jesus as "an inclusive symbol of God."[53] As in most liberal theology, Jesus is the *exemplar* of the faithful life.

It is also interesting to note what Howard Thurman does *not* claim for Jesus. The following statements are primarily derived from Thurman's silence on certain doctrines of Christianity. His treatment of the Christian festivals, which celebrate the life of Jesus, offers pertinent examples.

Howard Thurman never speaks of the birth

of Jesus in terminology rooted in the doctrine of Incarnation—the doctrine which stresses God's unique entry into history through the Christ child. The meaning of Christmas rests upon the irrefutable record that a life surrendered to God can have victory over the forces which stand against fulfillment. Thurman writes:

> After theology has done its work, after the reflective judgments of men from the heights and lonely retreats of privilege and security have wrought their perfect patterns, the birth of Jesus remains the symbol of the dignity and the inherent worthfulness of the common man.
>
> Stripped bare of art forms and liturgy, the literal substance of the story remains, Jesus Christ was born in a stable, he was born of humble parentage in surroundings that are the common lot of those who earn their living by the sweat of their brows. Nothing can rob the common man of this heritage—when he beholds Jesus, he sees in him the possibilities of life even for the humblest and dramatic a resolution of the meaning of God.[54]

Jesus is a symbol of the continuous possibility for newness which comes with each person.

Christmas has meaning, not because of a special birth, but because of a special life. Jesus so loved, he so intimately related to God, that men and women inevitably pursue his total history. Added inspiration comes in discovering that Jesus was born as they were born. Jesus is genuinely an example for the heights their life can attain.

Good Friday is not, for Thurman, an event which informs doctrines of atonement. Jesus is never mentioned as the sacrifice for humankind's sins. Thurman stresses two meanings of the crucifixion: 1) when Jesus cried out "My God! My God! Why hast thou forsaken me?" he declared the need to feel God's presence in that moment of terrible pain and anguish. Jesus wanted to be certain that the source of his life (God) was as available in this cataclysmic moment as during the other times of his life. In this cry Jesus again confesses his dependence upon God. Good Friday is a sign that life must ultimately rest, not in comfort, but in "commending our spirits" to God.⁵⁵ And 2) rather than the crucifixion being a God initiated event to redeem humankind, it is the logic of what happens to love in the world. To give one's self to God does not assure success, prosperity, or popularity. Since the social order contains evil, and since evil works against community, love faces immense difficulties. Good Friday is a statement about the nature of society, and the fate of the disciple of Jesus. Thurman affirms:

> The crucifixion of Jesus Christ reminds us once again of the penalty which any highly organized society

> exacts of those who violate its laws.
> . . . those who resist the established
> order because its requirements are
> too low, too unworthy of the highest
> and best in man.[56]

When Thurman speaks of Easter he talks about humanity's quest to affirm values and a quality of life which are not terminated by death.[57] He writes: "Perhaps the greatest discovery that we can make concerning Jesus is that, at long last, death could not touch in him that which gave to his life its great significance."[58] There is no affirmation of a bodily resurrection of Jesus, and its being a sign of eternal life. In realizing that the meaning of Jesus' life could not be killed and buried, that the essence of Jesus' life (the faith, love, and hope he manifested) remains alive and eternal in the world, one comes to know the reality of Easter.

Thurman does not speak of immortality as the preservation of personality after death. His only statement about a life after death is that the life which came from God (before birth) returns to God. Death is an event in this journey; it does not terminate the life's return to God, it does not terminate life. If Thurman had any notions about the nature of existence beyond the death event, he did not make them public.[59]

Communion becomes that meal which enables persons to realize their kinship under God. It confirms the spiritual bond of the social order. It acknowledges the power of love to give a meaning to life which is everlasting. This power and love are the same which informed the life of Jesus. In recognizing this link with Jesus, there is a sense of fellowship with him. This is the extent to which Jesus is part of the communion experience. Doctrines of transubstantiation and consubstantiation are not relevant to Thurman's theology.[60]

The concluding comment to be made about the significance of Jesus in Thurman's theology is: Jesus as life example is sufficient, but not absolute (final, the last word about the potential of personality). Jesus' example directs humanity toward community, it is an example of "the way" life should be committed. But even Jesus may have had a potential yet to be realized. Until his death, he may have been in the process of discovering more ways to further his spiritual development; his perfection may have been in the process of becoming. Consequently, there may be spiritual territory which is still to be covered by a seeker of God.

In an interview with Thurman, he shared this idea through the following illustration:

> Suppose you and I were standing on the ground, at the base of a ladder that went from the earth to the moon, and there were four or five people climbing. Now as we watched them, when the first person got out of sight, we would say, as far as

71

we're concerned, he's at the moon. But the man on the ladder that's climbing, about whom we're talking, knows that he may have 100 miles to go before he gets to the moon . . . . And this is what I think about Jesus. I think that as we stand and watch, he disappears; and we say he's there. But what I'm stupid enough to feel is that's not what he said. There's a long way to go before he gets there, and the higher we climb on that ladder, the more we see what I'm talking about; the longer we stay on the ground, the less we see, and that's why I feel—hit the ladder![61]

In Thurman's theology, Jesus shows the way to the source of life (God), but Jesus is not the source. He is the example which inspires, and not the perfected life to be worshipped and imitated. Thurman summarizes the way this idea is woven into his relationship with the life of Jesus, when he says, "I love him (Jesus), in no official way, no formal dogmatic way, but I love him as the guide and companion of my spirit who nudges me when I am making the wrong turn."[62]

The Nature of God

Only God is the source of life; and absoluteness belongs to God alone. These attributes emerge as one comes to understand the nature of God. This nature can be described as follows:

72

1. God is "the fact of life from which all other things take their meaning and reality."[63] God is the "ground of being." God is not only the Creator of animate and inanimate objects but also of life itself.[64]

2. God is near for "God has not left Himself without a witness in our spirits and in our lives."[65] Though Thurman, as all mystics, insists on the immanence of God in humankind and nature, his theology is not pantheism. He believes that "God must never be a prisoner in His creation."[66] Panentheism more accurately describes his thoughts on the presence of God; God is immanent and transcendent.[67]

3. God is personality. God is to be experienced as Father and Friend. This assertion is also part of the mystic's tradition. "Ultimate reality is personal," and is therefore approachable, understanding, and caring. God is not only near but intimate.[68]

4. God is love. God brings wholeness to all life. God endows the actualization of potential and the experience of fulfillment. God responds to life's basic need of being cared for. God breaks "the sense of isolation that the individual human spirit feels as it lives its way into life."[69] The love of God is omnipotent. No power can prevent it from ultimately achieving its will of unity and harmony in the universe.

5. God is universal. While the nearness of God is necessary, the om-

nipresence of God is also crucial (panentheism). "He [God] must be vast, limitless, transcendent, all-comprehensive, so that there is no thing that is outside the wide reaches of His apprehension."[70]

One of the important acts of God which emerges from this nature is that of judging. God is the One who assesses life and who punishes or rewards according to the merits of one's living. Cognizance of this function of God comes because the individual's personality is the medium through which it finds expression. God's immanence, God's investment in the individual personality, reveals meaning about creation. Thurman observes:

> But the fact remains that the judgment which the individual passes upon life and by which life weighs him in the balance, finds its key within the individual and not outside of him. It is the great and crowning dignity of human life. Man rates the risk that life takes by resting its case within his own spirit. How good God is to trust the Kingdom of Values to the discernment of the mind and spirit of man![71]

An important distinction must now be made between the ability of the individual to discern truth and the ability to judge life. The quoted statement and other remarks by Thurman speak to the necessity for the individual to accept his/her power to discern right from wrong. This acceptance means that one is responsible for one's decisions and actions. Morality depends upon responsibility. There is the threat, however, that men and women will not accept their finiteness and will deceive themselves into believing they have unerring ability and responsibility to judge others. This arrogance leads to playing God. The creature assumes the authority and power of the Creator. The ultimate judging of life must rest with God. Only God has the total vision of motive, cause, and consequence.[72]

Thurman acknowledges scriptural references to an eschatological final judgment day, but he does not assert this belief as part of his theology. He mentions the "Day of Reckoning" as an important concept which keeps the individual and community aware that they are accountable to God for their living. Though this "Day" among some religious traditions may mean a specific time for judging creation, for Thurman the time reference appears to be quite different.

Thurman's "Day" (in his normal use of language the word "moment" would be more appropriate) is that time when one's life comes before God for trial. While religious traditions profess this as an after death "Day," Thurman's moment can be during a person's lifetime. It is the awesome vision that one's life has been either lived in emptiness (damnation) or fullness (salvation). The vision is experienced as punishment or reward. Punishment (separateness from God) and reward (union with God) are present each moment as a life is either committed to isolation or community. Anticipation of the awesome vision should order a life for right living.[73]

The most important activity of God, however, is loving—God's caring for the individual and community. God's love gives definition to God's nature (Creator, Immanence, Personality, Universality). Love indicates how God's nature acts upon and through the universe, making unity out of disunity, harmony out of discord, order out of chaos, meaning out of meaninglessness, and hope out of despair.

God can only be known through love, and the fullest meaning of love can only be known through religious experience.[74] Thurman explains that "in the religious experience, the individual finds fulfilled what he has glimpsed in his other experiences of love: namely, that in the presence of his God he becomes aware of being dealt with totally."[75]

Religious Experience

Religious experience is defined by Thurman as "the conscious and direct exposure of the individual to God. Such an experience seems to the individual to be inclusive of all the meaning of his life— there is nothing that is not involved."[76] This "exposure" is necessary because *truth must*

76

be experienced. Truth is more than idea or belief; it is Reality. And the individual must encounter it, not only with the mind, but with the whole self.[77] Religious experience is the way to attain religious knowledge.[78]

The question of certainty arises at this point: certainty about the "experience" and certainty about the assumptions of "knowledge." It is helpful to distinguish Thurman's brand of mysticism from others which have a completely different position on this question of certainty. Douglas C. Macintosh, in his book, *The Problem of Religious Knowledge*, terms these other mystical theologies of religious knowledge as "extreme monistic realism." Extreme monistic realism is characterized by the conviction that God is a reality which exists "independently of all subjective human experience." Yet, God is sought and discovered in one's inner experience. The experience is not "mediated by representative ideas, but is direct and immediate." The experience is ineffable, but pure knowledge of God is received. God is perceived (by one's intuitive faculties) as so real that all matter, time-space relationships, self identity, and evil are unreal. God is the comprehensive, only reality. In knowing God, knowing the world (matter, time-space, self, society) is inconsequential. Or more precisely, knowing the world prevents one from experiencing the saving vision of God.[79]

Thurman's mysticism is better termed "critical monistic realism." Macintosh defines this as an experience where:

> Not all that is immediately experienced [i.e., God] in sense-perception is independently real, and not all that is independently real is immediately experienced by human subjects. . . . But it is possible to maintain that there is a core of existential or numerical identity, a partial identity or overlapping of the immediately experienced and the independently real. It is this partial identity or overlapping which makes verification possible.[80]

The mystic takes a "critical" look at his or her experience and recognizes that identity and interpretation are integral parts of it. The claim to pure knowledge of God is a deception.[81]

The title of Thurman's autobiography, *With Head and Heart*, is symbolic of this approach. The head utilizes reason, thought, and concept to interpret the heart's exposure to feeling, sensation, and experience. This is not done to demystify the mystery within religious experience, but to explore and appreciate the depths of mystery. Rather than certainty over pure knowledge of God, the mysticism of Thurman evokes assurance, awe, and wonder—sensations which are continually questioned and tested in order to attain some disclosure of God's will.

The other assertion of Thurman's mysticism, which differs from the "extreme" type, is that religious experience *affirms* rather than negates knowing the world. The vision of God gives a proper sense for the value of and need for one's commitment to society, matter, self, and the recognizing and fighting of evil. This particularly characterizes Christian mysticism which claims that moral-ethical insights emerge from mystical consciousness. The individual is therefore obligated to participate in transforming the environment to conform with the insights.[82]

Knowing the world is not only the *effect* of mystical consciousness but can also be its *source*. This is true for extrovertive mysticism. In his book, *The Teachings of Mystics*, Walter T. Stace explains:

> The extrovertive way looks outward and through the physical senses into the external world and finds the One there. The introvertive way turns inward introspectively, and finds the One at the bottom of the self, at the bottom of the human personality.[83]

Thurman's mysticism is "ambivertive"; that is, the introvertive and extrovertive approaches are useful to him.

The essential relationship between mystical consciousness and the world is evident in Thurman's understanding of the process by which religious experience effects a movement from self to God (another way of putting it would be from disunity to unity or from isolation to community). The basic process is as follows:

1. The individual has the sense that he or she is being encountered and loved in a personal and private way; a way which affirms one's ultimate worth as a child of God.[84]

2. The experience provides the "confidence of ultimate security." As Thurman states, "the human spirit is exposed to the kind of experience that is capable of providing an ultimate clue to all levels of reality, to all the dimensions of time, and to all aspects of faith and the manifestations therein."[85]

3. The experience of God gives life a new focus, a new sense of commitment. The subject realizes that only a life fully surrendered to God can experience meaning, security, and hope. God becomes the Absolute to which the life is given.[86]

4. The new life commitment (conversion) changes the character and habits of the person. Emotionally, spiritually, and physically the individual experiences more power to respond to the demands of life. The release of this power gives the individual an awareness of his/her potential for fulfillment, for love. The urge to be "Godlike" (perfect) transforms the personality to expressing fuller meanings of love.[87]

5. In expressing the fuller meanings of love, the subject seeks to change the social order. "In his effort to achieve the good he [the mystic] finds that he must be responsive to human

80

need by which he is surrounded, particularly the kind of human need in which the sufferers are victims of circumstances over which, as individuals, they have no control, circumstances that are not responsive to the exercise of an individual will however good and however perfect."[88]

6. The transformation of the self and the social order discloses community (salvation). A life which responds to the vision of God (religious experience) will establish the kind of relationships where God is experienced more and more, and where the underlying unity of reality becomes the (immediate) environment in which society finds itself."[89]

Thurman believes that the Christian has in Jesus the example of how mysticism informs the good life—the life which finds fulfillment from religious experience. Thurman interprets Jesus' baptism event as one which triggered mystical consciousness. The event set in motion the process which has just been outlined:

1. Jesus had the personal sense of being God's child. He heard a voice from heaven say, "Thou art my beloved son, with thee I am well pleased." (Mark 1:11)

2. Jesus rushed into the desert to understand the new commitment his life must take. In the desert he was confronted with temptations to betray his vision. His mind challenged him to

test the vision by defying the natural laws (jumping from the temple); to test the vision by taking political leadership and establishing the righteous kingdom (denying God to become ruler over the earth). Jesus emerged from these temptations with a deeper sense of God as the ultimate source of his well-being, the ultimate source of order through the natural laws, and the ultimate source for righteousness. Jesus knew God as the ground of life.[90]

3. The experience of self and God led to a new life commitment. Jesus began a ministry which continuously attested to the fact that life must be surrendered to God.

4. Power came to Jesus. In his presence people were healed of the limited lives they had lived. Jesus recognized that his power was of God. In expressing this power he allowed God to be manifested through him.

5. The religion of Jesus aimed at changing the social order. It not only gave the "disinherited" a survival technique, but a new sense of the power of love which is able to transform all things.

6. The disciples and the lives of people he encountered became Jesus' "test group" where he was able to see the ability of love to form community. Jesus' claims for the establishment of a new kingdom were testimony to his faith in the destiny of love to rule relationships.

The disciplines which aided Jesus in the development of his religious knowledge are always available to people. These disciplines are commitment, growth (developing a sense of self), love, suffering, and prayer. Except for prayer, these disciplines have already been discussed. Attention is therefore given to the meaning of prayer in religious experience.[91]

Thurman defines prayer as:

> . . . the method by which the individual makes his way to the temple of quiet within his own spirit and the *activity* of his spirit within its walls. Prayer is not only the participation in communication with God in the encounter of religious experience, but is also the 'readying' of the spirit for such communication.[92]

The individual has the ability and responsibility to condition his/her self for religious experience. And yet, Thurman does not believe that one can control, manipulate, or predictably initiate the experience; these powers belong to God. The mystic can lay no claim to making the experience. The person does not earn or merit it. The experience is a gift of God, an example of God's grace which comes to humanity.[93]

Through prayer, the person acknowledges dependence upon the gift. The person hopes to demonstrate his/her willingness and readiness to receive it. It is a way in which the person not only becomes primed for the experience but is able to procure its fullest meaning. Prayer is the central discipline for knowing God and the ordering of life because of the experience with God.

The Inclusive Church

The Church is important to Howard Thurman because it is Christianity's "trustee" of religious experience.[94] Thurman has a deep concern about the Church's commitment to this high calling. This concern grows out of his analysis of the Church's record with this responsibility. Denominationalism and sectarianism have not just arisen to meet the varied expectations for religious experience, but have emerged because of bitter theological arguments and social and economic prejudices. Rather than being symbols for the richness of diversity and pluralism, they symbolize the fragmentation caused by intolerance, oppression, and alienation.

Churches have too often been established out of an *ethos* of exclusion: excluding those who do not believe specific dogma, and excluding those who believe the accepted dogma but who are of a particular socio-economic status.[95] Thurman believes that as long as the Church operates on the principle of exclusion, it cannot faithfully be the trustee of religious experience.

Religious experience is an including experience; it takes in God who is all in all. Its essence is love which continually seeks and nourishes wider expressions of itself. The excluding character of many churches is antithetical to the nature of religious experience.[96]

Howard Thurman is convinced that a significant aspect of this problem resides in the fact that Christians have not correctly understood and faithfully followed the Church's central figure, Jesus. Jesus so adequately expresses the love-ethic that churches have evidently lost sight of his life and teachings.[97]

Thurman's focus on Jesus does not mean, as in many churches, that Jesus should be worshipped. Jesus should be known as an example for the needs of individuals. He demonstrated a proper sense of self. He experienced God. He committed his life to the vision of God. He loved all with whom he came in contact. And he helped create community. This life, says Thurman, is ". . . the source of inspiration and humiliation. Inspiration, because in him we see what is possible for human beings to attain. Humiliation because we have so much and we do so little with it."[98]

The practical consideration here is that Jesus as life example is a unifying principle. It should satisfy the basic affirmation of Christians and not offend (perhaps even appeal to) non-Christians. Jesus as religious object (God) excludes those who cannot make this proclamation, who have come to know God through some other great teacher. So for Thurman, the deification of

Jesus is not only theologically unsound, but contrary to the community building mission of the Church.[99]

God is to be the only object of worship for the Church. God is the most inclusive symbol and reality for religious experience. Thurman goes so far as to state that the Christian Church experiences completeness when members of other faith claims are an integral part of its fellowship. The true Christian Church is the one which includes all who seek God and offer a commitment of their life to God. The experience of knowing God and the inclusive fellowship, professes Thurman, is "the way" of Jesus; they are therefore, Christian.[100]

The life of Jesus is a (not *the*) particular expression of religion which, when followed, lifts the spirit to new heights. The Bible is a collection of books which reveals the drama of God making covenant with a people (Israel), and the prophetic interpretation of the meaning of this relationship given through the teachings and person of Jesus.[101] Jesus and the Bible, according to Thurman, are not the final source of authority for religion. They are a particular way to the authority.

The larger rubric which encompasses their purpose to the individual is religious experience. Through examination of their (Jesus and the Bible) story, the imperative of a right relationship with God becomes starkly real. The final source of authority is the religious experience where God is encountered. With religious experience as the final authority, the Church should not limit its sources of religious insight to Jesus and the Bible. Other religions' faith claims, materials from the arts, and any discovery which opens a door to knowing God are useful to Christian nurture.

To Howard Thurman this is not syncretism, it is not diluting the meaning and power of Jesus, Christianity, and the Church. Quite the contrary, it is a faithful witness to what Jesus and the truth upon which he founded his Church were all about. It is the *essence* of Christianity.[102]

This essence shapes the work of the Church in two basic ways: 1) the individual should be given a greater sense of self and the spiritual resources which nourish the personality; and 2) the person should feel equipped to live morally and ethically in the social order. Manifestations of love should increase within the institution and in all places where the institution and its people find themselves. The Christian Church should discover that it is including more and more people and concerns, which are outside its fellowship, within its loving circle. This means that the Church confronts all barriers to community. Prejudice, discrimination, segregation, the absence of help for the poor and oppressed, and the abuse of civil rights become targets for the Church's mission.[103]

Howard Thurman expresses a deep loyalty to the institutional Church. His attestations about religious experience have not resulted in the criticism, which is often directed at mystics, that he is apathetic toward the life of the institutional Church. Thurman's loyalty is not manifest in his labor for denominational structures, nor in fostering continuity with historical Church traditions and practices, but in: 1) his sharp criticism of the institution, 2) his proclamation of a vision for the Church to become its original ideal, and most important of all, 3) his participation in that vision through a ministry in an institutional church. In these ways his message and style is characteristic of the Hebrew prophets who continually called their people back to the essential vision of covenant with God. Standing within the Church, Thurman announces that it has a tradition of universalism which must be honored if "the Church is to be the Church."[104]

God is searching for a witness through which God can find expression. If the Church fails to serve in this capacity, Thurman believes that its life is not assured. God is not dependent upon the Church.[105] It is to the Church's credit that it has a tradition, ethos, and authority (in God) which consecrate it to meet the demands for community. It is Thurman's ardent and prophetic plea that the Church accept its high calling and become a saving (community making) institution. In doing this, it will find its own salvation.

Thurman and Liberalism

Roots and Branches

The preceding outline of Howard Thurman's theology lodges him within the traditions of mysticism and romanticism. Though mysticism is his primary tradition, romanticist philosophy informs his thinking on many crucial concerns.[106] Both of these traditions are part of the rubric of evangelical liberalism. One discovers that Thurman's thinking is connected with the evangelical liberalism of his mentors (Cross, Robins and Jones). Many of his ideas are their ideas, or at least one can say, representative ideas from their tradition.

This connection still does not make the classification of Thurman an easy affair. First of all, evangelical liberalism (as well as mysticism and romanticism) is a complex tradition which contains varied expressions that are not always compatible. There are particular kinds of mystics, romanticists, and evangelical liberals. Secondly, all of Thurman's ideas do not completely fit within evangelical liberalism. Major aspects of his theology require another category. Classifying always oversimplifies—partly due to the inadequacy of labels, and partly the dynamic quality of mind which refuses to follow the script of any one system.

Howard Thurman and his mentors make almost identical comments on the significance of the human personality, life of the spirit, love-ethic, nature and meaning of Jesus as life example, necessity for religious experience, ultimate devotion to God, relatedness of all life, judgment, challenge before the Church, and the power within religion to build the Kingdom of God (community) as a personal and social reality. Their distinct areas of emphases were delineated in the previous chapter. Two critical concepts emerge, however, on which there is considerable variance between Thurman and his teachers. These concepts deal with the source of religious authority (particularly as it relates to Jesus and the Bible) and the vision of ultimate community.

Cross, Robins, and Jones make Jesus the supreme revelation for religion. Jesus is the most perfect and ideal example for all humanity. George Cross states that because of Jesus, humanity knows more about God's character. It is therefore possible to say that Jesus "is Lord and God to us." Cross goes on to say that Christianity is the culminating faith for world religions. Other religions are "Christianity in its beginning or lower stages." Christianity can, therefore, include all the world's peoples. It can and must be "committed to the conquest of the world."[107]

Rufus Jones refers to Jesus as "the supreme revelation of the ages," "the (Adam) type at last fully expressed." And before the Jerusalem Meeting of the International Missionary Council, Jones says that Christianity can "win the world" if Christians truly witness to their faith, for "everybody admits without question or debate that the Galilean way of life is the most beautiful ideal that has yet been proposed."[108]

Henry Robins, among the three men, has the most extreme position about the authority for Christianity. Not only does he argue for Jesus' sinlessness, but says that "Jesus was not simply supreme exemplification of faith, but was himself its object." Though all authority is of God, for the Christian, final authority is "of God in Christ." Religious experience is totally dependent upon the Bible, for the Bible reveals Christ.[109] Robins claims Christianity to be one of the world's greatest missionary religions. Its mission is to help build the Kingdom of God. Robins's writings indicate that his understanding of the establishment of the Kingdom of God in the world is synonymous with the establishment of a Christian social order. Or as Robins terms it, "the Kingdom of the Son of His love!"[110]

These statements by Cross, Jones, and Robins on Jesus and the missionary motive of Christianity are integral to the *essence* of *their* Christian faith; *they are integral to evangelical liberalism*. Howard Thurman's Christian essence rejects these concepts. His understanding of Jesus falls more in the tradition of "modernistic liberalism." Kenneth Cauthen describes the stance of modernistic liberals:

> The thinking of these men was not Christocentric. Jesus was important—and even unique—because he illustrated truths and values which are universally relevant. However, these truths and values can be validated and even discovered apart from Jesus. He is not so much the *source* as he is the *exemplar* of the religious norm. Jesus might be psychologically helpful, but he was not usually thought to be logically necessary for the highest experience of God in human life.[111]

Thurman holds that the source of the faith's authority is in the individual's experience of God rather than in worship of Jesus.

The authority question also raises a point of difference as Cross, Robins, and Jones develop their thought around the life and teachings of Jesus as recorded in the Scriptures. While Thurman also relies heavily on Jesus' example, he readily uses autobiography, philosophy, psychology, history, literature and other disciplines to verify the truth of Christianity. One of his axiomatic expressions is "what is true in any religion is to be found in that religion because it is true, it is not true because it is found in that religion."[112]

Again, Thurman's approach is more in the tradition of modernistic liberalism. The modernistic liberals are characterized by their methodology which avoided the necessity to "appeal to some external authority [i.e., the Bible or Christian tradition] which had to be accepted on faith."[113] They strove to discern religious truth by using the empirical disciplines.

Howard Thurman's mysticism (critical monistic realism) is also an empirical theology. The experience of God is tested. It submits, even longs, for verification. Religious truth is pursued through life experiences and concepts of reality.

The essence of evangelical liberalism affirms a religious teleology in which Christianity wins the world to profess Jesus Christ as Lord. The saved community is the Christian community. The Kingdom of God is more precisely the Kingdom of God in Christ. Christianity's goal is to convert individuals and societies to "the way" of Jesus; any achievement less than this is inadequate.

Thurman believes that Jesus as the "object" of religious experience is a dividing rather than uniting principle—it works against community, against love abiding as a saving force for the world.[115] Thurman is not talking about a "post-Christian epoch." He asserts that a religious fellowship maintains the essence of Christianity when it professes "the way" of Jesus and not the way of Christian dogma. The participants who are not Christian do not become honorary Christians, neither do they lose their identity to a transcendent new religion, but they affirm the universal which they have come to know in a particular way.

In a conversation with Thurman he told

me that he was not interested in converting people of other religious faiths to Christianity. He felt that it was crucial for people to discover their religious heritage and affirm its revelation of the Divine. Before deciding to abandon one faith for another, persons must know what it means to live faithfully within their religious tradition. Thurman's success in communicating the necessity for devotion to religious roots is attested to by Rabbi Joseph Glaser when he credits Thurman and two rabbis as the men who "opened my Jewish eyes for me in a way no one ever had, and few have since."[116]

Paul Tillich addresses the concern for particularity and universality in his *Christianity and the Encounter of the World Religions*. He says:

> . . . Christianity will be a bearer of the religious answer as long as it breaks through its own particularity.
>
> The way to achieve this is not to relinquish one's religious tradition for the sake of a universal concept which would be nothing but a concept. The way is to penetrate into the depth of one's own religion, in devotion, thought and action. In the depth of every living religion there is a point at which the religion itself loses its importance, and that to which it points breaks through its particularity, elevating it to spiritual freedom and with it to a vision of the spiritual presence in other expressions of the ultimate meaning

of man's existence.[117]

In this way Howard Thurman is a Christian and universalist. His universalism is an expression of his Christianity.

Evangelical and modernistic liberalism have many common characteristics. Persons within the liberal tradition, therefore, will probably have concepts which find a home in both types. The authority of Jesus and the Bible, and the mission of the Christian faith become decisive criteria. They put Howard Thurman more suitably within the tradition of modernistic liberalism. Considering the relatedness of evangelical and modernistic liberalism, Thurman's theology is not a radical break with his mentors, but a significant departure upon which he stakes his claim for developing his thought and work.

Bearing Fruit

In conversations with scholars I have discovered that Howard Thurman's ideas are not wholeheartedly accepted. A major criticism focuses on the central theme throughout his theology: the concept of community. One criticism of the community concept relates to Thurman's stress on unity. The question arises: at what point does unity deny identity?

In Thurman's writings he clearly states that community should affirm identity, while insisting that persons seek a new identity of

oneness with their fellows and the universe.[118] This could appear as a contradiction
which attempts to reconcile distinct unrecon-
cilable objectives. One must either seek to
build personal identity or forfeit it to the
larger group.

The criticism has specifically been applied
in questioning the Christian character of
Thurman's theology. I have heard persons
accuse Thurman of being so syncretistic in
developing his ideas that he has lost the
unique message of the Christian Gospel.

Thurman's theology can be attacked by
those convinced that identity is based upon
pure and distinct beliefs or conditions.
Emphasizing unity, ecumenism, or universalism are viewed as weakening identity
building, and the weakening of identity is
viewed as prohibiting persons from understanding their witness to the ultimate truth
through a *unique* mission in life.

Union can threaten, negate, and destroy
identity. Howard Thurman, however, is
speaking to a different process of unity—a
process which affirms identity and unity.
The individual's personality is not melted
into a group personality. People do not
become colorless or without distinct cultural
qualities. Rather than sameness, Thurman's
community is a sense of inter-relatedness
and inter-dependence. Identity is not static,
but a growth process whereby the individual
becomes aware of his or her membership in
larger categories of life (i.e., male or
female, family, tribe, society, and race).[119]

Only in affirming one's *inherent relatedness* to others will the proper sense of self (identity) be realized. The consciousness of relatedness should include more of life in one's loving circle. As the individual's sense of identity grows, so does one's sense of responsibility. The child may only care for himself or herself, but it will eventually become responsible for family and society.

Thurman's concept of community does not belittle the importance of identity. What Thurman does assert is the affirmation of a personal identity which enables one to affirm an identity with all life. The essence of personal identity is the essence for identity with the universe. The essence of Christian identity is the essence of all religious life. Essence is not diluted, compromised, impotent characteristics which are the least common denominator for the particular and general. Essence is the core qualities which give concentrated, inexorable, and potent definition to the self and its relation to others.

The profitable argument with Thurman might center on what he considers this essence to be, not that he belittles identity. Thurman's "essence" might be too stripped of essentials. No doubt orthodox Christians and many social radicals would be quick to point out the errors of his reductionism. Ignoring identity would be the kind of negligence which reflects on Thurman's relevance and sensitivity. Acknowledging his sensitivity to identity, however, moves the

97

discourse to a more productive level. Differences about the makeup of identity are the basis for constructive debate with Thurman.

The identity-community relationship was not just a theological concept for Thurman, but the basis for his creative impact upon American life. The term "creative" is being used as defined in Earl H. Brill's *The Creative Edge of American Protestantism*. Brill describes the "creative edge" as "that segment of the Protestant community which, at any given time, is most aware of the realities of the social situation and which seeks to bring to bear upon that situation the insights and concerns of the Christian faith."[120] Thurman's ministry corresponded to this definition along two main rubrics.

First, he was one of the most prolific interpreters of the life of the spirit. His writings, hundreds of lectures, meditation tapes, media programs, teaching positions, and chapel deanships provided numerous opportunities for his influence to be felt. In these opportunities Thurman addressed, as counseled by George Cross, the hunger of the spirit.

This rubric is an important contribution to pastoral theology. Pastoral theology being the undergirding theology for what ministers do. This theology defines religious identity within the various roles and functions of ministry. In churches, hospitals, the military, community centers, and educational institutions, clergy are called upon to offer counseling, preaching, community organization, and other approaches which respond to their people's needs. This work, when properly done, is not just problem-solving but caring. A caring which addresses the deepest level of identity: the spirit. A caring which emanates from devotion to God.

Thurman's theology focuses on the dynamics of the spirit—a focus which gives significant insights to pastoral theology. He identifies spiritual crises and ecstasies which determine how life is valued and lived. He illuminates the spirit's journey and its process of finding fulfillment. And most important, he leads people to insights which nourish and empower their spiritual well-being. Thurman's theology asserts the necessity for persons to have a proper sense of self, to know their identity as creatures of infinite worth (who I am), and to know their identity as children of God (whose I am). He addresses the most fundamental need of the personality, that is, a healthy sense of identity.

Though his insights are useful to pastoral theology, Thurman did not develop them with professional clergy in mind. His primary audience was laity. He exhorted them to recognize their prophetic power and the supreme joy of a life committed to their prophetic vision. With God as the omnipotent, omniscient, and omnipresent source of love, the individual has available a resource of power which enables the fulfillment of personality. This power not only permits self-affirmation, but it gives the personality the potential to shape a loving reality (community).

In many ways Thurman's theology resembles that of Ralph Waldo Emerson. The rejection of dogma in order to discover truth in nature, the belief in humanity's divinity, the emphasis upon the individual, the commitment to mysticism, and the certainty regarding the possibilities for community are primary in their thought.

These romanticist concepts feed what some consider as Americans' spirit of optimism.[121] Being a country founded on the belief that it was a New Eden for God's Kingdom, a society which viewed its frontier as an opportunity for bettering one's condition, a culture whose expectations for improved life-styles increased with technological advances, and a people convinced that divine providence determined their mission to be like "a city upon a hill" to the world, the bases for an optimistic outlook became an integral part of the American experience. Liberal theology, with its belief in the essential goodness of humanity and unlimited possibility in realizing human potential, reinforced the optimism—an optimism which was a dominant trait in the American character. Irving N. Bartlett says that Emerson's popularity was due to an ability to address this American trait and need. In the nineteenth century "Americans were ready to believe in their own divinity"[122]

This analysis perhaps explains Thurman's influence during the twentieth century. He touched this same need of the American people and gave reassurance of their worth, mission, and capability. Thurman's commitment to the realization of the loving community, and his emphasis on the individual's role in shaping it, are concepts rooted in nineteenth century romanticism. His representation of this tradition could lead one to characterize him as the Emerson of the twentieth century. This does not mean that Thurman merely restates Emerson's ideas, but he creatively appropriates the same basic philosophy to his time and circumstances.

The difference of time and circumstance results in insights which Emerson never fully treated. Thurman as a black man in America had a "point of view" which eluded Emerson and other romanticists. Thurman knew the reality of racism as evil, the necessity for community concepts which included black people, the importance of the historical Jesus to the disinherited, and the importance of social mechanisms in the achievement of justice.

Another comparison which may lend some help in interpreting his creative contribution in the field of spirituality, is to compare him with other religious thinkers in this field. Thurman's concept of community, as mentioned previously, grows from the mystical and romanticist notion of a harmonious universe. Sydney E. Ahlstrom, in his book, *A Religious History of the American People*, charts the various religious groups, leaders, and movements which are also rooted in this tradition. He labels this religious outgrowth as "harmonial religion." Ahlstrom defines this expression as follows:

> Harmonial religion encompasses those forms of piety and belief in which spiritual composure, physical health, and even economic well-being are understood to flow from a person's rapport with the cosmos. Human beatitude and immortality are believed to depend to a great degree on one's being 'in tune with the infinite.'[123]

Aspects of this religious expression are particularly found in Mary Baker Eddy's science of health, Ralph Waldo Emerson's transcendentalism, Bruce Barton's Jesus as the successful business executive, Norman Vincent Peale's positive thinking, and most recently, in the emergence of growth centers which believe that life can be controlled through meditation and the proper cosmic consciousness (a kind of spiritual magic).

Substitute in Ahlstrom's definition the word "God" for "cosmos" and this formula is also evident in some charismatics: "have enough faith and be healed."[124] The message from these groups is that happiness, wealth, health, success, and fame not only "flow from a person's rapport with the cosmos [God]," but *they are the purpose* of rapport with the cosmos (God).

Howard Thurman's theology has a very

different focus. While he concedes that God consciousness yields power, the intent of this power is to serve God and not the individual's well-being. Thurman does not deprecate well-being, but serving God may mean a vow of poverty, risking health, experiencing pain, suffering, ostracism, and death (as it did with Jesus). Serving means discovering peace, not as the world defines it, but a "peace which passes all understanding."

Again, Thurman's involvement in America's race problem gives a key to understanding his difference with harmonial religion. He recognizes the dangers in identifying the circumstances of a person's life as evidence for one's spirituality. This test always results in the poor/oppressed and the rich/oppressors meriting their conditions. Thurman argues that God's beloved children are not defined by their socio-economic status. This would deny their innate infinite worth.

Jesus is a model for this principle. His is not a rags to riches story (as in Bruce Barton's account of Jesus in *The Man Nobody Knows*), neither is he the winner of a popularity contest, but Jesus is God's beloved Son because of his faithfulness to the vision of Love. Likewise, black Americans cannot be defined by their socio-economic conditions for they have innate worth. Neither does their salvation hinge on release from these conditions, but in their ability to express love as an affirmation of their worth. Here the influence of Nancy Ambrose is strongly felt. Her story about being in slave conditions, yet maintaining the status as God's child, furnishes the generating principle of this idea.

Evil cannot just be understood as a disharmony within the spirit of the subject—a disharmony where right adjustment disputes the presence of evil. Thurman was aware that evil may originate from the social order and affect the innocent. The black experience of oppression does not originate with a defect in black people but in the oppressive character of white society.[125]

This led Thurman to a greater social change commitment than one finds in representatives of harmonial religion—social change which implements justice, equality, and other safeguards for human rights. He was not just concerned with God, but community rapport with God. Among American pietists, Thurman is a leading protagonist of the demand of religion for transformation of the socio-political structures of society.

Thurman's theology and ministry have kept the existential reality and suffering of black people before America. The motif of *freedom* in his thought can be understood as informing his liberalism—that is, freedom from orthodox theologies which confine the basis of authority and quests of his mind. The freedom motif is integral to his spirituality which insists upon the eternal possibility for one to experience integrity and hope despite limiting conditions. But included in the motif is not only religious freedom, but social freedom. Any precept or action which inhibits the realization of one's full potential must be eliminated. And the plight of black Americans is a central concern of his prophetic witness.

The race issue in America as a primary context for doing theology is the second major rubric which denotes Thurman's creative impact. Here again his grandmother's influence is marked. Whatever religion says about life, it must include a loving response to the circumstance of being black in America. As a black person who experienced alienation, suffering, humiliation, and hostility from the social order, Thurman knew the inescapable urgency for shaping a theology which challenged the social order which perpetrated these indignities. His social position gave him a sensitivity which utilized romanticist philosophy as a remedy for the social and spiritual problems of the twentieth century—a sensitivity which identified race relations as one of the century's major social and spiritual problems.

Combatting racism, as Brill states in his book, is one of the most challenging "creative edges" for the mission of Christianity. Yet, it has been ignored by theologians as a crucial issue for theology, or test for the Christian movement and the establishment of the Kingdom of God.[126] Howard Thurman has been the most prolific theologian on this creative edge. His

explication of the identity-community correlate regarding race relations is a signal
contribution to America's religious thought
and life. The next chapter examines his
prophetic witness to this concern.

Chapter IV

THE PROPHETIC WITNESS

Howard Thurman understood racism to be a "contradiction of life." Racism is inimical to the formation of identity. Neither blacks nor whites can attain a proper sense of self and give full expression to their potential in an environment of prejudice, segregation, and violence. Racism is inimical to the formation of community. Systematic discrimination sabotages the function of community as a place of nurture and growth through cooperation. Destructive forces are released that rupture life's inherent inter-relatedness.

Thurman felt victimized by racism. He was acutely aware that it attacked his self worth and freedom. It attacked the well-being of community. His mystical experiences provided the assurance that he was a beloved child of God, and that harmonious relatedness is the underlying structure of reality. Racism denied the truth about God's intent for creation. It put the welfare of the community in crisis. The prophetic questions became: How could he help shape a social reality that conformed to his religious knowledge? How could he speak to the crisis by restoring the community's (especially America) sense of well-being?[1]

The Message

The Example of Jesus

One of Thurman's first published writings dealt with the person and meaning of Jesus. In 1935 his article "Good News for the Underprivileged" outlined the ideals which would later be more fully treated in his classic, *Jesus and the Disinherited*.[2] In these writings Thurman is attempting to define the religion of Jesus as the essence of Christianity. He emphasizes the social circumstances of this poor and oppressed Jew, and then concludes that the religion of Jesus was a creative response which emerged from and dealt with transforming these conditions.

Thurman is adamant in keeping Jesus as a member of the disinherited and not just as one who ministered unto them. Jesus was a victim of oppression. His message of deliverance was not from one who stood outside the suffering but from one who was subject to it. His religion was the life saving resource for people who were poor, dispossessed, and oppressed. They were treated as aliens in their own land, without justice or any legal sanctions which recognized their right to decent and fair treatment. His religion was a resource for people whose dignity and integrity fell

108

under such violent assaults that they stood "with their backs against the wall."[3] Jesus, Thurman believes, was giving the Jewish people a religious resource to save their sense of self and to help them begin experiencing the Kingdom of God (community). The religion of Jesus is therefore a religion specifically aimed at empowering the disinherited.

It is significant to note that Thurman begins his writing career by clarifying the meaning and purpose of the faith's central figure, Jesus. The historical Jesus is essential to Thurman's theology. The activity of Jesus within his social environment provides crucial insights to understanding his meaning for humanity. Jesus is Christianity's exemplar because of the way he (being fully human) was able to reveal God's truth within and about the human condition. This was a truth which affirmed justice and righteousness, the dignity of all people, the necessity for love to rule all relationships, and the power of love to overcome evil and create community. Only when one embraces the historical Jesus are these political implications recognized as inherent in Christianity's essence. Through the historical Jesus, God's identification with and empowerment of the disinherited becomes evident.

Thurman then makes an analogy which had not been used among theologians when he says:

> The striking similarity between the
> social position of Jesus in Palestine
> and that of the vast majority of
> American Negroes is obvious to
> anyone who tarries long over the
> facts. We are dealing here with con-
> ditions that produce essentially the
> same psychology.[4]

This unique connection results in two major conclusions: 1) the socio-economic-political status of Jesus most closely corresponds to the socio-economic-political status of the American Negro; and 2) since Christianity is essentially a religion of and for the disinherited, it is appropriately a religion of and for the Negro.

These conclusions completely upset a norm for much of American theology and religion which have assumed that Jesus' life and ministry more closely resembled the status and values of privileged, white Americans.[5] A further extension of this norm's ethnocentric and class biased orientation is seen in American civil religion where Christianity is synonymous with "the American way" (i.e., democracy, capitalism, legal-socio-economic policies).[6] The perspective of this theology is that of the privileged and fully enfranchised. Religion becomes a sanctioning force for their socio-political status and values—a religion of and for the inherited.

This has seriously affected the sensitivity which theologians bring to the plight of black Americans. The predominant response of theologians has been to overlook the black situation as a context for the application of their theological insights and discourses. The black condition did not register as one which merited consideration for testing the moral society. Consequently, all kinds of atrocities were perpetrated upon blacks (i.e., slavery, lynchings, segregation, discrimination, and denial of civil rights), and the resulting circumstances were not understood as critical to the work of Christian theology. Even if theologians had a personal concern for American blacks, their absence of theological reflection on blacks' life crises must be interpreted to mean that the black condition was not considered determinative in the making of the moral society. The society could be racist and Christian.

It is not difficult to see the next stages of brutality which can conceivably grow from this insensitive attitude. Christianity not only ignores these atrocities, it condones them as means for advancing the faith. Slavery becomes a God-ordained, and therefore Christian, institution. The subjugation and extermination of blacks receives religious sanction (as witnessed in the Ku Klux Klan's creed of Christian allegiance).[7] Biblical arguments are made to prove the inferiority of blacks. Again, Christianity becomes a religion of the ruling powers, of those who seek to control the lives of the weak, poor, and oppressed.

Another response of theologians has been to proclaim the obligation of privileged

Christians to minister to the disinherited. This ministry has often been construed as a mission to lift the disinherited to higher levels of faith and salvation. The truth of God is perceived as coming to the unfortunate through the fortunate. The dispossessed are saved by the wisdom, power, commitment, and virtue of the ruling class. This attitude of white Christians made Thurman "suspicious" of anything related to missions. Too often, he believed, the missionary has felt superior to the non-Christian, ignoring his or her innate worth and the worth of a non-Christian culture. It is this prevailing *ethos* in missionary work which breeds racism and segregation.[8] The disinherited are primarily the "objects" of Christian mission, the recipients of Christian good-will.[9]

Howard Thurman's interpretation of the relationship of Jesus and the disinherited counters these historical scenarios. Jesus, and therefore Christianity, is not to be identified as siding with the slave-master but with the slave, not with the political decision makers but with the disenfranchised, not with the acceptable but with the despised, not with the socially privileged but with the oppressed, not with the comfortable but with the suffering, not with the powerful but with the weak. In connecting the condition of Jesus to that of the American black, Thurman is calling these other scenarios heresies to the essence of Christianity. Thurman reclaims the Jesus of and for the disinherited.

This interpretation has profound implications for Christian race relations. In ignoring and oppressing blacks, American religionists have ignored and oppressed the group of people who reveal in distinctive ways the truth of Jesus. Thurman writes:

> How a man describes his belief in God when his life is serene and his place and position are safe and secure may differ radically from what he has to say when the storm is raging and the winds are wild and unrestrained. It is my conviction that what a man has to say about the meaning of God when he lives in a society which he largely controls and in which he is accepted may be quite different from what he has to say about the same God if he lives in a society in which he is always marginal and of no account. It is for this reason that I am convinced that the test of any religion, as far as its impact upon mankind is concerned, turns on what word does it have to share about God with men who are the disinherited, the outsiders, the fringe dwellers removed from the citadels of power and control in the society.[10]

White people can no longer relate to black people as if they are their spiritual superiors whose role is that of missionary or mentor. Blacks have in the religion of Jesus a message which affirms their worth as inheritors of a truth about God's power and action. Whites can learn from and be evangelized by the spirituality which is found in the black religious experience.

God empowers the disinherited to create God's community of love. God reveals God's self in a special way to those who have no resource or recourse other than God to meet the harsh demands of life.

Thurman does not consider blacks to be spiritually superior to whites. They do not have an "elect" status before God. But blacks live under the kinds of circumstances where they have a different experience of God's love and power. They *know*, like no one else can know, how thoroughly God identifies with all their needs. It is this unique perspective that provides an understanding which usually escapes the privileged and anyone else who is insensitive to the plight of blacks. Suffering can yield spiritual insight and growth. It is therefore the American Negro, Thurman says, who offers a vital witness to the power, activity, and will of God. The Negro offers a vital witness to the expression of faith, hope, and love which are necessary for the creation of God's kingdom. The Negro offers a vital witness to the religion of Jesus, the essence of Christianity.

The Testimony of the Spirituals

Howard Thurman uncovers evidence for his convictions about black Americans and religion in his interpretation of the Negro spirituals. The spirituals are songs which communicate the sorrows and lament which the slaves felt for their condition. They are also songs of protest against inhumane circumstances and songs of comfort which enabled the slaves to endure tremendous suffering and indignities. The slaves had developed a profound theology which spoke to their existential situation. The slave songs did not just carry political, psychological, musical, or social responses to their condition, but a rich religious understanding of existence.

Thurman rediscovers a theological tradition which has been ignored as making any contribution to America's religious heritage. One of the most significant theological expressions in America's history is made through the spirituals, and Thurman helps define its meaning. In evaluating their importance he says:

> For these slave singers such a view [that ultimate meaning was limited to one's immediate experiences in life] was completely unsatisfactory and it was therefore thoroughly and decisively rejected. And this is the miracle of their achievement causing them to take their place alongside the great creative religious thinkers of the human race. They made a worthless life, the life of chattel property a mere thing, a body, *worth living!* [11]

He is one of the first writers to explicate

the theological significance of these slave songs. His creative contribution reveals the ability of the slaves to experience and understand the power of God as the ground of their life and hope. The slaves had discovered that the heart of Christianity spoke lovingly to their condition—that the religion of Jesus provided a proper "sense of self," identifying them as children of God, as a people of ultimate worth.

Thurman's work with spirituals cites such topics as death, evil, life, meaning, heaven, Jesus, God, religious experience, nature, hope, process, time, the Bible, salvation, and justice as concerns which are treated in these songs and developed in a way which assured the slave of God's love, righteousness, and power for their ultimate destiny. The spirituals attest to the genius of the slaves to discover the survival function of Christianity.

Thurman's treatment of the spirituals indicates his interest in discovering religious and theological resources within the tradition of the Negro folk. If God's truth is to and in the midst of the disinherited, then one should find evidence of God's "Word" dwelling among them. The spirituals are testimony to the presence of God's truth finding new expression through the faith of these oppressed people.

Thurman's two books which are full treatments of Negro spirituals are *Deep River* (1945) and *The Negro Spiritual Speaks of Life and Death* (1947).[12] One can see that

116

Howard Thurman's early writings are addressing the activity of God among and for black people in America. They are addressing what religion has to say to *his* situation as a black man in America. This social witness of Thurman's follows the process of his theology. That is, the first step is for one to develop a proper sense of self, a proper understanding of who he or she is in relation to God. Knowing Jesus' relationships to the disinherited, and God's assurance to his (Thurman's) disinherited forebears (the slaves), Thurman is able to develop a vision of community with self confidence about his worth within that vision.

After this affirmation concerning the worth, contributions, and significance of black Americans, Thurman develops a concept of community which grows from his racial identity and religious beliefs. Since his understanding of a universal community has already been given attention, the following pages deal more specifically with his perception of Christian community and American community, and how these particular expressions of community find a fulfillment which is consistent with "the underlying unity of life."

Crisis in Community

A proper relationship with blacks is a basic tenet of Thurman's concept of community. Christian community, therefore, cannot accept racism. Thurman believes that segregation and its attendant ills cause moral irresponsibility. The Christian faith cannot thrive in that kind of atmosphere, for the "genius of the Gospel" affirms integration.[13]

Integration does not mean there is magic in whites and blacks being physically present to one another, for Thurman states: "hatred often begins in a situation in which there is contact without fellowship, contact that is devoid of any of the primary overtures of warmth and fellow-feeling and genuineness."[14] Without fellowship one tends to be unsympethetic to the full humanity of another; it is difficult to feel another person's needs and complete range of emotions which shape the personality. Losing the full sense of another's humanity is to lose the sense of another's ultimate worth, and to place him or her outside one's ethical field. The outsider becomes less than human and can therefore be treated in inhumane ways. With this occurrence, the hope for reconciliation is lost. Integration is a call for primary fellowship, and therefore reconciliation, and therefore community,

The concept behind Thurman's use of the term "fellowship" is explicated by Henry Nelson Wieman. Wieman distinguishes "sympathetic" and "instrumental" association from "organic" association. Sympathetic association is defined as "one in which the people associated share the same feelings, the same

118

thoughts, the same aspirations, the same hopes and purposes."[15] Instrumental association is one in which persons work together in order to provide charitable services for others. It is organic association, however, which describes what Thurman means by "fellowship."

In organic association possessing the same feelings, interest, thoughts, and purpose is *not* essential. Persons may differ significantly on issues, but through the fellowship, members develop an appreciation of other perspectives while finding their own nurtured by the contact. Service is not excluded from organic association. Its purpose is to create the environment which makes organic interaction possible. Since, as Thurman believes, the universe is by nature organic, this type of fellowship is the only kind which produces harmonious living. Through organic fellowship inter-relatedness and reconciliation are discovered. Organic fellowship is synonymous with Thurman's concept of community.

Another catastrophe which arises from segregation is the way it results in blacks and whites losing a proper sense of self. Thurman describes the effect upon many blacks as follows:

> The real evil of segregation is the imposition of self-rejection! It settles upon the individual a status which announces to all and sundry that he is of limited worth as a human

> being. It rings him round with a
> circle of shame and humiliation. It
> binds his children with a climate of
> no-accountness as a part of their
> earliest experience of the self. Thus
> it renders them cripples, often for the
> length and breadth of their days.[16]

This strips a person of his or her human freedom, and freedom is essential to moral responsibility. Thurman goes further to say that denying this freedom is not only immoral, but since it ignores a person's "birthright" (the gift given him/her by God) segregation must be viewed as "an act against God."[17] For blacks who have a strong sense of self, segregation too often drains their emotional, physical, and intellectual energy from concerns of creativity to those of survival. In these ways the oppressed are kept from realizing their full potential. Where one's potential is stymied, full community is not possible for anyone, black or white.[18]

White persons lose a proper sense of self when the laws and customs of segregation cause them to feel superior to black persons. If they see blacks as children of God, they see themselves as "favored" children of God. The sense of true kinship between blacks and whites is therefore broken and proper inter-relatedness is lost. The creative energy of many whites is diverted to defending a malevolent social structure, and their full potential is also not realized. They do not fully experience or contribute toward community.[19]

Thurman criticizes the Christian Church as a supporter of *limited* community. It has done this through racial separation, which is prevalent in Church life, and through its zeal to identify the "saved" and the "damned." Separating and categorizing eventually lead one group of people to feel morally superior to another. When this mood infiltrates a group, conditions are set for an hostility which only works for limited community.[20]

Since Christian community is formed and nourished by the love-ethic, opportunities must be established for people to be in primary fellowship in order to express love and to be loved. Thurman says:

> It is necessary, therefore, for the privileged and the underprivileged to work on the common environment for the purpose of providing normal experiences of fellowship. This is one very important reason for the insistence that segregation is a complete ethical and moral evil. Whatever it may do for those who dwell on either side of the wall, one thing is certain: it poisons all normal contacts of those persons involved. The first step toward love is a common sharing of a sense of mutual worth and value.[21]

This is where Thurman feels the Christian Church has such a great opportunity and responsibility. It has the ethic, the informing beliefs, and the calling to establish a loving, inclusive, inter-racial environment. This is the only hope for community. Thurman makes harmonious race relations a fundamental component to the creation of Christian community. He ties this necessity to the very essence of the Christian faith and the Church's mission.

Howard Thurman maintains the same philosophy regarding the establishment of community in America. If the nation is to realize its potential for community, it must cherish the full citizenship rights of black Americans. This is the only way national unity and morality can exist.

Thurman believes that America was founded upon a principle of community. It had a unique historical role as a nation where God had a new opportunity to establish community.[22] His ideas fit the concept of America as the "new Eden," the place where the past did not hamper fresh beginnings. The future was open. Prejudices, customs, and traditions did not prevent the actualizing of social and political ideals.[23] In this setting Thurman places a people who had a political sense of equality which is consistent with his definition of the Christian sense of kinship. He says:

> . . . that there is inherent in the American dream, rooted in the insight, that there is an equality that is not built upon learning, upon training, upon status, upon wealth or lack of wealth, or privilege or lack of

privilege, but a quality that each man recognizes when he feels as he experiences life, that this is not life in general, this is my life. When a man feels that he himself, in and of himself, without reference to any pretension whatsoever, that he is of worth beyond value. And when in a society we call out from other men as we meet them, this which announces that the sense of infinite worth and value, which I know applies to myself, I affirm that it applies to you.[24]

He believes that America was established upon a vision which conforms to life's urge for community. Its political and social ideals, as articulated in *The Constitution* and *Declaration of Independence*, recognized individual worth and the importance of reconciliation as community-making principles for the social order. The *essence* of American ideals considers black Americans as equal and vital members of the nation's life and future.

The integrity and well-being of the nation may rest with its treatment of minorities, with its commitment to its original ideals, and with its commitment to full community. Thurman gives a specific example of this notion:

. . . it is quite possible that in the major struggle between the Soviet Union and the United States of America the future belongs to that power which is the most convincing witness to the fact that it makes

123

> available to all its citizens the freedom
> of access to a social climate in which
> the individual not only has an
> authentic sense of belonging, but in
> which it is a reasonable hope for him
> to actualize his potential, thereby expe-
> riencing community within himself as
> part and parcel of the experience of
> community within the state. [25]

Thurman's concern for community in America is expressed in his 1946 article "The Fascist Masquerade." Here he identifies three American groups (Christian American, The Nationalists, the Ku Klux Klan) which were actively racist. Since they advocated segregation as a binding principle for American life, Thurman considers them a threat to the social order. These organizations fuse Christian principles and America's founding ideals with their racist ideals. This is particularly dangerous "because it gives to any current doctrine of racial inequality or superiority a new dimension of dignity and respectability."[26]

This is why it is so important for the bases of American community and Christian community to be grounded in principles which support the creation of universal community and reconciliation between *all persons* in creation. Life will only support those movements which work toward total harmonious relations within the universe. Here again, Thurman makes harmonious race relations essential to both Christianity's and America's hope for community, and the fulfillment of a cosmic teleology toward community.

The Response of Religion

Thurman is convinced that religion is the catalyst for realizing full community. Religion is not orthodoxy or political theology, but the all-embracing spiritual dimension of life which commits the individual to worship of and service for God. The religious life is the ethical life, but it is also more; for life is not assessed just on the human condition and human values, but on its relationship to God's judgment. Thurman says that when this happens, "things are no longer merely ethical or unethical, they are sinful or righteous—a religious quality has appeared in morality."[27]

Spirituality does not just consider the "ought-ness" (ethics) of helping to form community, but the fact that participation in this labor enables one to experience God. Service to others yields religious experience. Social change can possibly make the opportunity for religious experience available to those who find their energies siphoned into securing themselves against a hostile environment.[28] All situations are perceived as encouraging or preventing religious experience. Life is described as supporting or opposing the spiritual journey. Here ultimate meaning is read into social, economic, and political structures. They are not just responsible to local or national or international standards, but to God's concern for unity.

Thurman can, therefore, make the statement that segregation is at its "root" the presence of evil in the human spirit. This is a significant analysis by Thurman in that it makes the relationship with blacks an important criterion by which the spiritual health of a people is judged. Segregation is not just immoral or unlawful or unjust, but sinful and an affront to God. The designation by Thurman makes race relations an ultimate concern for religion.[29]

Howard Thurman challenges Christians to bring their faith to bear on race relations. This is not only necessary for resolving racial problems, but for Christianity to contain a religious quality. Thurman asserts that Christianity is only religious insofar as it gives a person the sense of his or her ultimate meaning and value. This means that faith must be actively involved in transforming American society so that racial barriers, which prevent true assessments of worth, are destroyed.[30]

As mentioned earlier, the Church bears the responsibility to be a primary force in fighting segregation and forming community. He feels the Church's ministers are called to provide the leadership which helps the Church remain faithful to its ideals. In his commencement address to graduating clergy of Garrett Biblical Institute he says:

126

> As prophets of the most High God, it
> is your divine assignment to announce
> that man lives his days under the per-
> sistent scrutiny of God—that God is at
> stake in man's day. How men treat
> each other, what they do to the en-
> vironment in which little children must
> grow and develop, how they earn their
> living—all things in the making of
> which they play a significant part
> stand bare before the eyes of God.
> You must live and proclaim a faith
> that will make men affirm themselves
> and their fellowmen as children of
> God. You must lay your lives on the
> altar of social change so that wherever
> you are there the Kingdom of God is
> at hand! [31]

This conviction is specifically related to race relations in his article "The Christian Minister and the Desegregation Decision"; here black and white clergy are challenged and provided approaches to establish the creative unity which should characterize society.[32]

In his effort to confront Christians with the principles of their faith, as they relate to race relations, Thurman calls upon whites to: 1) relinquish their position of privilege where all the formal power, which operates the society, resides among white Americans, 2) not just work for good within the system of segregation, but to attack the system itself, 3) be totally committed to integration, to see their destiny as tied to the destiny of blacks, and 4) to create the kinds of fellowship with blacks so there is mutual understanding and respect.[33] These changes will not just improve the plight of black Americans, but they will free whites from fear, hate, a false sense of pride, and defensive techniques which cause them to lose initiative over their lives and which prevent the nourishing of the spirit.

In some ways segregation is more harmful to its perpetrators than to its victims.[34] In this analysis Thurman not only ties integration to the demands of the love-ethic, but to the self-interest impulses of the personality. The self can only find fulfillment in a loving community, and a loving community is only possible when the individual selves are given the opportunity for their fullest possible nurture and expression.

Wholeness, the urge for unity, harmonious inter-relatedness are innate self-interest drives of every organism. If whites therefore deny integration, they are going against the key to their own salvation. Thurman has consequently formulated an argument for white involvement in the processes of integration which does not just appeal to good will or moral responsibility or Christian principles or political ideals, but to white society's concern for white society. The Christian faith's stand on the side of integration is in the best interest of blacks and whites.

Howard Thurman's social witness can also be interpreted as a challenge to black

Americans to recognize the significance of the Christian faith as the basis for social transformation. He believes that in Jesus, blacks have the example of the possibility of liberation from a condition of oppression. The religion of Jesus not only points to the source of power for the oppressed, but the basis of their identity and worth. The witness of the slaves, through the spirituals, is the historical evidence for the capability of Christianity to meet the needs of the black condition. The love-ethic is able to overcome fear and hatred. It can form the community which affirms the full personhood of blacks.

Thurman strongly rejects any concept of community which calls for separation from whites. Whites should not be perceived as inhuman (outside the realm of ethical responsibility) nor as the perennial enemy. Thurman admits that racial separation may often meet two basic requirements of community: 1) a sense of identity with a race, cause, and purpose (the bases for cooperative action), and 2) the feeling of membership with others of common values, with whom there is the experience of direct and intense communication.[35] But separation ultimately leads to a limited community, a community which does not conform to the unity demanded by Christian faith and the teleology of life.

Full community is necessary if blacks are to develop their full potential, for it has been limited community which has historically prevented blacks from full rights and privileges. Thurman writes:

> There are many who have lived deep in the heart of American society and know with certainty that to undertake to build community as a closed entity within the large society is not only suicidal but the sheerest stupidity, because it plays directly into the hands of those persons and elements in society who have stood as defenders against any and all inclusiveness as the true [American] basis of community.[36]

The protection and preservation of individual or racial identity is a crucial concern for Thurman. He believes, however, that identity can be developed and nourished without separation. Integration does not mean that blacks give up their "blackness" but that they affirm their oneness with all humanity.[37]

The call for blacks to labor for inter-racial fellowship is not just to provide whites with the kind of understanding which will enable them to fight segregation. It is not just so blacks will have partners in the struggle for justice and equality. But it is for the well-being of the spirit of black folk. Thurman surmises that the absence of a loving fellowship produces a milieu for hatred, not only for whites to hate blacks, but for blacks to hate whites. And hatred rots the spirit.[38]

130

Here Thurman completes the spiritual significance of integration. Inter-racial cooperation has political, psychological, and sociological merits, but he provides a unique treatment which considers the religious merits and implications of integration. The spiritual welfare of the social order depends upon the initiatives which are made for an inter-racial community.

Howard Thurman goes further to stress that blacks must take the initiative for inter-racial relations. Again one sees him rejecting the assumption that white society is the salvation of black society—that within white society there is the power to free blacks from oppression. He believes that blacks have the resources to meet the demands of their ultimate destiny. God *directly* empowers their cause and equips them to love and form community.

Thurman's insight from mystical experience informs his philosophy for social change. That is, within each individual is the presence and power of the divine providing ultimate meaning and ability to transform external circumstances. Blacks can keep the initiative over their lives by taking the lead in race relations or they can forfeit this initiative to white society.[39] He emphasizes that the oppressed must liberate themselves. Whites play a critical role in the liberating process. They help create the climate and mechanisms for change. But liberation must be initiated by those who best know the suffering of oppression and urgency for freedom. The act of initiative itself is a statement about the underprivileged's capability to take charge of their lives and to set the terms for their future. It is a statement about the underprivileged's equality of inherent worth and power with the privileged.

The Ethic of Nonviolence

This forming of full community requires an aggressive approach to the problem of segregation. Thurman says: "Preaching to such persons, in my opinion, is apt to be a waste of effort and is a blind alley. Some method must be achieved by which the sufferers in the situation can act to shock the oppressor into a state of upheaval and insecurity."[40] The rationale for this "shock" treatment is explained as a means:

> . . . to tear men free from their alignments to the evil way, to free them so that they may be given an immediate sense of acute insecurity and out of the depths of their insecurity be forced to see their kinship with the weak and the insecure. Men do not voluntarily relinquish their hold on their place. It is not until something becomes movable in the situation that men are spiritually prepared to apply Christian idealism to un-ideal and un-christian situations.[41]

This is where Thurman suggests nonviolent protests (i.e., boycotts, non-cooperation, demonstrations, sit-ins) as the key means to provide the shock and transform the social order. The development of a philosophy of nonviolent protest for the black struggle is a foremost achievement of his social witness.

Here Thurman makes a signal contribution to providing a method for change in American race relations. He has done more than any other person to articulate the *ethical* and *spiritual* necessity for blacks' civil liberties struggle to be grounded in the principles of nonviolence.

As early as 1928 in his article, "Peace Tactics and a Racial Minority," Thurman begins to outline how a "philosophy of pacifism" can begin to eliminate whites' will to control and blacks' will to hate. Very little is said about techniques of interaction or confrontation. His primary concern is to call a truce to attitudes which promote separation.[42] He begins to outline more fully the basic principles of his nonviolence ethic in the early part of 1935 at the annual convocation on preaching at the School of Theology of Boston University. This material is later developed into the book *Jesus and the Disinherited*.[43] In these writings Thurman examines the necessity of nonviolence under the term "love-ethic." He concludes that love is the force which creates full community, and nonviolent change is the best expression of love.

His *Disciplines of the Spirit* (1963) goes further to explain how he links nonviolence to the spiritual quest for wholeness.[44] Since the will to segregate is a spiritual problem, only a spiritual answer which affirms the binding attributes of love will suffice. Violence is the act through which the nonexistence of the other person is willed, with hate as the dynamic. At the same time this is an act of self-affirmation, for hate becomes a "man's way of saying that he is present." Ultimately, the human spirit cannot tolerate this because it denies the elemental truth of life that "men are made for each other." Violence is in opposition to the "fact of the underlying unity of life." Violence is in opposition to full community.[45]

Nonviolence responds in a caring way to the perpetrator of violence. It announces that the well-being of the individuals involved is of ultimate concern. It moves the level of confrontation to a higher spiritual plane. Instead of merely defeating one's offender physically or psychologically, one begins to create the climate for love to be a force which has to be dealt with in the relationship. The presence of loving care introduces new possibilities for reconciliation. Only nonviolence permits love to enter conflict creatively and address the prevailing spiritual ills of separation, fear, and hatred.

Thurman's commitment to nonviolence is not just because of its capacity to accomplish his social ends; he advocates nonviolence on moral and spiritual grounds. Only when the spiritual dimension is addressed is there any real change with ultimate meaning and movement toward God's community.

To see the uniqueness of Thurman's thought, a helpful comparison can be made with James Weldon Johnson, the Field Secretary of the National Association for the Advancement of Colored People between 1915-1930. Johnson was also a spokesman for nonviolence during the period when Thurman was developing his nonviolence philosophy. His concept of community and inter-racial cooperation is based on a practical technique for black improvement. Johnson does not believe that inter-racial cooperation is a matter of "brotherly love or any of the other humanitarian shibboleths"; he feels that "common sense" dictates inter-racial contact.[46]

Johnson does not consider physical force a viable option for blacks in their struggle. He does not dismiss it on moral grounds, for he believes that physical force is a "rightful recourse of oppressed peoples."[47] It is to be rejected because it would not help blacks to achieve their goals. Lacking arms and numbers of people, blacks would not have a chance of winning their struggle through violence.

Thurman would criticize Johnson's rationale for not using physical force as a renunciation with only tactical significance. He explains its shortcomings in saying:

> Here nonviolence may be used effectively by violent men as a practical

135

necessity. In this sense it has the same moral basis as violence. This is one of the ancient weapons of the weak against the strong and is part of the over-all tactic of deception. It is instructive to note that when noviolence [sic] is used in this way in response to external necessity, this may not at all vitiate its creative impact upon those against whom it is used. The importance of this cannot be overemphasized. Because nonviolence is an affirmation of the *existence* of the man of violent deeds, in contradistinction to the fact that violence embodies a will to *nonexistence*, the moral impact which nonviolence carries may potentially realize itself in a given situation by rendering the violent act ineffective and bringing about the profoundest kind of change in attitude.[46]

The familiar question, "do the ends justify the means?" is answered by Thurman with a resounding "no!" The loving community of justice and equality can only be attained by loving means. Community cannot be built on hate or the tools of hate.

Even suffering can be a nonviolent means for establishing a more acceptable climate for reconciliation. Suffering can be redemptive in a situation of violence. By redemptive Thurman does not mean that black suffering expiates the sins of whites— the stains of evil are not sacrificially removed. Suffering does not sanctify blacks or atone for whites' evil. It is redemptive in that it furthers unity rather than brokenness. It provides the needed time, consciousness, or atmosphere for a more creative and caring response than violence. Suffering manifests a higher truth: that even the threat of death is not as compelling as the necessity for love.

Thurman's nonviolence convictions are definitely based upon his interpretation of the Christian faith. Jesus, in *Jesus and the Disinherited*, is perceived as one who confronts and transforms evil to good through utilization of the love-ethic. A nonviolent philosophy and activity characterized his ministry. He revealed God's will for human interaction. Nonviolence is viewed as affirming the existence of one's enemy, and therefore affirming life, and therefore affirming God. Violence works for the nonexistence of the enemy, and therefore repudiates life and God.

It must be remembered that Thurman's theology primarily develops from his personal experiences. His convictions are not adopted systems of belief, but convictions which have been shaped, tested, and proved within life experiences. He requires empirical evidence for his beliefs. Several occurrences can be credited with informing his nonviolence philosophy. In a 1936 visit with Mahatma Gandhi, Thurman was extremely impressed with Gandhi's ideas on the power of nonviolence as a method which positively responds to the spiritual needs of humanity, while at the same time accomplishing the necessary political transformation of the social order.[49] Certainly, Gandhi's success in India was solid evidence for nonviolence. Gandhi reinforced, confirmed, and provided deeper insights about nonviolence, but Thurman's basic convictions were well established before the 1936 trip.

The 1929 internship with Rufus Jones could also be interpreted as a time when Thurman became indoctrinated on pacifism and the vital social witness which had been performed by Quakers. But Thurman had joined the Fellowship of Reconciliation in 1922, an organization dedicated to resolving wars and social conflict by nonviolent means. This membership indicates that his commitment to pacifism preceded the relationship with Jones.

The root context of his convictions may be a situation which occurred during his childhood. After fighting another boy, he went home bruised and tattered. As he faced his grandmother the following exchange took place:

> "No one ever wins a fight," were her only words as she looked at me. "But I beat him," I said. "Yes, but look at you. You beat him, but you will learn someday that nobody ever wins a fight."[50]

Thurman then says that Nancy Ambrose's words have helped him to see, throughout all his years, the futility of violence, be it in resolving personal problems or world wars. So, while his commitment to nonviolence is an act of faith, it is also grounded in a history of experiences which empirically indicate the creative alternative of nonviolence.

Thurman's concept of community ties the black struggle for freedom to divine will and destiny. The black struggle becomes a holy struggle. In defining the ethic of nonviolence, he gives the freedom movement a holy mechanism. Now placed in the hands of the weak is not only a vision of their journey's goal, but a method which blesses the pilgrimage itself. Nonviolence, like the effect of mystical consciousness, gives one the opportunity immediately to experience an ultimate truth (love) in the midst of suffering.

This identification of Thurman as the creative mind behind the development of a philosophy of nonviolence for the black struggle underscores the significant contribution of his social witness. The beginning of a philosophy of nonviolence in the civil rights struggle of black Americans is often traced to Martin Luther King, Jr. and the Montgomery boycott of 1954. Although the boycott may represent the most successful and notable application of this philosophy, nonviolence received considerable discussion and shaping in the 1930's.

Black leaders such as Adam Clayton Powell, Jr., W.E.B. DuBois, Asa Phillip

Randolf, and James Weldon Johnson did not consider physical force as a viable option for blacks. Theirs was a political, and unlike Thurman's, not an ethical rationale for non-violence. Reinhold Niebuhr made a passing reference to the issue of blacks and nonviolence in 1932; he too spoke to the concern as a matter of social and political strategy.[51] The emphasis upon a nonviolent ethic for blacks is not extensively dealt with by anyone, except Howard Thurman, until the advent of King in the 1950's.

S.P. Fullwinder suggests in his book, *The Mind and Mood of Black America,* that Howard Thurman may have been the first person to plant the "seed of nonviolent suffering" in the Negro mind.[52] He goes further to credit Thurman as indirectly responsible for introducing Martin Luther King, Jr. to the nonviolent ethic. Fullwinder suggests that Thurman may have interested Mordecai Johnson, then President of Howard University, in the ethical significance of Gandhi's nonviolence philosophy for blacks. After Johnson made a pilgrimage to see Gandhi, he too began to spread the word on the nonviolence ethic. In King's *Stride Toward Freedom* it is stated that he (King) began seriously to study the usefulness of the non-violence ethic after hearing Johnson lecture on Gandhi.[53]

Historian Lerone Bennett, Jr., while interviewing Martin Luther King, Jr. during the 1956 Montgomery boycott, noticed Thurman's *Jesus and the Disinherited* in King's brief-

140

case. Considering that King was supposed to have plunged deeply into Gandhism as the boycott wore on, it is interesting to speculate about the possibilities of Thurman's influence.[54]

Hanes Walton, Jr., in his *The Political Philosophy of Martin Luther King, Jr.* also sees the nonviolence ethic being developed by Thurman and picked up by Mordecai Johnson. The primary distinction which Walton makes between Thurman, Johnson, and King is that Thurman and Johnson are expounders of an idea, while King is its practitioner.[55] As long as the term "practitioner" is understood to mean one who mobilizes a mass social movement, Walton's distinction is correct. Thurman does, however, *practice* the love-ethic within his arena of ministry. He does have significance as an expounder *and* practitioner.

Testing the Vision

Howard Thurman's ministry was dedicated to revealing the possibilities for community. In characterizing his work, the motifs of experimentation and model building continually emerge. His mind and life were oriented to *test* insights received from his religious experiences. The fundamental insight was the assurance of God's love, which expresses itself as affirmation for the individual and reconciliation in community.

Thurman, like Mahatma Gandhi, believed that truth has to be experienced. Where the proper setting is absent, one must create the setting for an experience to verify or negate the truths upon which a life is founded. In positions from Oberlin to Boston, religious programming was designed to demonstrate that a loving fellowship, where individuals sense their common ground with others, is more compelling than experiences of separation. Fellowship Church was perhaps the principal context that served as a crucible for his religious convictions.

Fellowship Church was organized as an inter-racial and inter-cultural congregation. When Thurman became its minister in 1944 he perceived that the opportunity had become available to give form and content to his message on the possibility and value of inclusive community. The membership and programs of the fledgling congregation grew under his leadership.

For Thurman, Fellowship Church was a religious and not just a social experiment. This is evident in Thurman's statement: "The experience of worship became the keystone of the entire structure. My basic concern was the deepening of the spiritual life of the gathered people."[56] Throughout the descriptions of his work at Fellowship Church, he emphasizes the development of a religious idiom that enabled people from various religious traditions to have a common experience of God's loving presence. This receives as much attention as the inter-racial and inter-cultural character of the church. The church's worship and programs were geared to help persons discover the essence of religious experience—an essence not dependent upon denomination, creed, or dogma. One can easily understand how such a religious ethos was compatible with Thurman's liberal theology.

The adequacy of the religious experience, generated by worship and programs, would have to be verified by more than the *feelings* of members. The proof for adequacy would be in the way social relations were altered to reflect the experience's religious insights. This occurred in two ways. One, the members of Fellowship Church began to have significant exchanges of fellowship and caring in one another's lives—exchanges between persons of various racial and ethnic groups.[57] These exchanges proved the ability of sensitive presence (fellowship characterized by understanding and caring) to form community. Two, the church affected the larger society through the social transformation activities of its individual members. As stated earlier, Thurman's ecclesiology did not call for the involvement of Fellowship Church (as an institution) in the politics of society, but aimed to empower individuals to address economic, political, and social needs.

Thurman writes:

> The core of my preaching has always concerned itself with the development of the inner resources needed for the creation of a friendly world of

friendly men. . . . It was my conviction and determination that the church would be a resource for activists—a mission fundamentally perceived. To me it was important that individuals who were in the thick of the struggle for social change would be able to find renewal and fresh courage in the spiritual resources of the church.[58]

This approach is consistent with the identity-community correlate in Thurman's thought. The individual is the key to community formation, and community provides the context to nurture and assert identity.

Fellowship Church received national acclaim for its example in race relations. The church became a model of possibility for churches nonplussed and paralyzed by social diversity. It became a model of Christian witness for a pluralistic society. Through Fellowship Church, Thurman proved the inclusive genius of Christianity. The church provided the empirical evidence he needed to confirm the insights from his own mystical consciousness about life's teleology toward community. The experiment of Fellowship Church verified the ability of Christianity and its institution to be a conduit which is capable of exposing and effectively addressing major contradictions of life, especially racism.

Rebuttals

Love and Justice

A basic concept upon which Thurman's theology is founded stresses the transformation of society through the transformation of individuals. Like many pietists, Thurman believes that change in the social order is contingent upon individuals changing their attitudes and actions which collectively determine the social order.

This concept is often illustrated by Thurman in his use of T.R. Glover's *Christ in the Ancient World*. Glover hypothesizes that the Roman Empire collapsed because the average Roman citizen lost his and her sense of importance to and responsibility for the Empire. The analysis does not deal with major economic and political forces which affected such a complex world state, but with the individual's attitude within the state.[59] The spiritual impoverishment which comes from an improper sense of self is perceived as the cause for moral decay in the society. And where individuals have a proper sense of self, the stage is set for strong moral forces to shape a moral and secure society.

This reasoning faces sharp criticism by the noted theologian, Reinhold Niebuhr, who continually spoke to the "defects" in Christian liberalism. Niebuhr, in his book, *Moral Man and Immoral Society*, argues that the ethical considerations which govern

145

relations between individuals are not the same as those which govern inter-group relations. One may be willing to make all kinds of *personal* sacrifice to live the ethical life (moral man), but the same sacrifice may be too much to ask of a body politic (immoral society). As an individual, one may have the right to face emaciating and abusive conditions as a symbol of protest against policies, but the same individual may decide that a more violent response is required if those conditions threaten his/her fellows. A group is not just the sum total of its individual members. A group can have a consciousness and value system which differ from those of its individual members.[60]

When this problem was posed to Thurman, he admitted the difficulties which arise in his moral position. He stated that while he might be certain about a nonviolent response to an act of violence perpetrated against him, he might react differently if his wife were in the same danger.[61] Niebuhr's thesis raises serious dilemmas for Thurman's focus on the ethical individual as the key to the ethical society. The ethical individual may be very responsible in interpersonal relations, and be ill-prepared to be the ethical political leader or other decision maker for the society.

Thurman is *not* insensitive to this problem. In speaking to the necessity for mysticism, he cautions: "the problems of human relations can never be solved merely by the radical transformation of individuals in society."[62] Though he acknowledges the power of social structures in determining the quality of existence, *the individual is still perceived as the key to remaking the social structure, and love as the ruling ethic for remaking the individual.*

In contrast to Thurman's love-ethic, Niebuhr believes life must not only be governed by a concept of love but also by a distinct and profound concept of justice.[63] There are situations where concepts of good-will and caring for others do not shed light on mitigating exploitive, explosive, and destructive circumstances. Justice recognizes the inherent danger when power and opportunity are stripped from one people and reside completely with another.

The work of justice does not separate itself from the interests and work of love. Niebuhr believes that justice can be a fulfillment of love; he says: "Yet the law of love is involved in all approximations of justice, not only as the source of the norms of justice, but as an ultimate perspective by which their limitations are discovered."[64] It is necessary, however, to understand how justice manifests itself as a particular expression of love—an expression that may not comply with expectations placed upon the love-ethic which operates in relations between individuals.

Howard Thurman recognizes the distinction which must be made between love and justice. In his Eden Theological Seminary lectures on "Mysticism and Social Change," and in his sermon entitled "Justice and Mercy," he discusses the importance of shared social power as a mechanism for the fulfillment of love.[65] In these discussions he still concludes that the love-ethic can contribute the moral force required for the social order.

Niebuhr's analysis raises legitimate questions on the realism of developing a social construct which depends upon an interpersonal love-ethic—questions to which Thurman's work does not give sufficient attention. It can be argued that Thurman's vision is noble, but it has an unrealistic means. The struggle for justice may be a more appropriate concept for achieving community than the ethic of love.

Violence and Love

This distinction between an individual ethic and a collective ethic, between a personally oriented theology and a socially oriented theology, becomes particularly evident when one deals with Thurman's belief in nonviolence. Even he admits that the nonviolence ethic may be inoperative in certain contexts:

> Unless the actual status of a human being as such is denied, reconciliation between people always has a chance to be effective. But when this

148

> status is denied, a major reappraisal
> or reassessment must take place *be-*
> *fore* the work of reconciliation—
> which is the logic of nonviolence—
> can become effective.[66]

Thurman believes nonviolence is moral when it is "redemptive," when it is able to "find a way to honor what is deepest in one person and to have that person honor what is deepest in the other."[67] This contingency presents multifarious dilemmas for the use of nonviolence. How does one determine the possibilities for redemption and the redemptive method? Is it not possible that violence may at times be a better expression of love than nonviolence?

George Cross, Thurman's seminary professor, speaks to this concern in saying:

> But when a time comes when violence offered to a man on account of his faith is recognized as unjust, and when the Christian allows his assailant at all times to go unscathed in reputation and unpunished in body, he may be doing the community, the assailant, and himself a great wrong.[68]

Reinhold Niebuhr also argues the difficulty which a nonviolence ethic carries in asserting itself as Christian or as a necessary tool of justice. Niebuhr writes: "They [liberals] will find nothing in the gospels which justifies nonviolent resistence as an instrument of love perfectionism."[69] Nonviolence as *an* (not *the*) expression of love, as a redemptive moral force which is not used as often as it could or should be, is a major contribution to instilling the religious factor in social transformation.[70] The redemptive necessity, however, prevents nonviolence from being an absolute. The relativity of nonviolence is not as fully treated by Thurman as one might expect.

A specific context for discussing this issue is the revolution which led to the founding of the People's Republic of China. In a land where millions of people suffered inhumane social conditions, Mao Tse-tung successfully engineered a revolution which greatly improved the life of the dispossessed. The ideas behind this transformation stand in sharp contrast to Thurman's philosophy, yet these were the ideas which supported perhaps the only possible way for the change to occur. In his book, *Love and Struggle in Mao's Thought*, Raymond L. Whitehead notes that Mao understood revolution to depend more on the elimination of class distinctions than working to fulfill a principle of "universal love." It is on this point, that Mao felt liberalism was the enemy of revolution.[71]

This does not mean that Mao abandoned a concept of love, but the concept only had meaning as it related to the elimination of class distinctions and their attendant injustices. In this justice struggle, violence was inevitable if powerful class groups were to be forced to surrender control over weaker classes. Power only yields to power, and the only kind of power which some groups recognize is violence. A nonviolent approach would play directly into the wishes of dominant groups which have little conscience about the suffering of the oppressed. Revolutionary violence is not an end, but at times the only means to achieve justice.

The advocates of nonviolence are quick to point out the successes of their method in the face of overwhelming odds. Richard B. Gregg's classic book, *The Power of Nonviolence,* begins by enumerating the various situations in which nonviolence overcame oppressive power: Hungary's nineteenth century conflict with Austria, the Indians in South Africa who during the turn of this century fought for civil liberties, Gandhi's renowned confrontation with the British for India's independence, Denmark and Norway's refusal to yield to Nazi rule, and the civil rights movement in the United States.[72]

The counter to this argument centers on a determination of the possibilities for nonviolence to affect those who control power. There are political situations where nonviolence has some chance to transform a dehumanizing social order, and there are other situations where it has zero potential as an instrument of change. Saul Alinsky, who is acclaimed for his skills and accomplishments in community organizing,

151

analyzes Gandhi's struggle for independence as one which carefully assessed the possibilities for nonviolence to be a force for change. The assessment was not done in a vacuum, based upon moral principles, but measured the personality, principles, and political philosophy of the opponent.[73]

Colin Morris, in his book, *Unyoung—Uncolored—Unpoor*, makes the same point as Alinsky. After discussing Gandhi's pragmatic approach to using nonviolence, and indicating how the British government was susceptible to this method, Morris says:

> Ruthless modern despots do not play good-natured games with their critics. It is hard to imagine Hitler or Stalin blenching at the prospect of Gandhi fasting to death. They would have helped him on his way, exterminating him secretly so that there was no mark of his passing except for a bloodstain on some cellar wall. Had Gandhi been got rid of in this way, the moral value of his sacrifice might still stand for all time, but its political significance would have shrunk to nothing. People who vanish without trace do not make effective rallying-points for freedom.[74]

Morris's primary involvement is with the oppressive conditions of blacks in South Africa. He concludes that the regimes of Rhodesia and South Africa are so entrenched in their racism and political control that nonviolence would have no effect in furthering justice. Violence must be an option. And for Morris the consideration of violence is not a relinquishing of Christian principles, but a faithful response to them. Violence, he believes, can be an expression of Christianity's love-ethic.

In considering political situations like China and South Africa the necessity for a concept of justice becomes all the more obvious. Justice provides a better conceptual framework for confronting oppressive and repressive national politics. It dictates corrective action though the consequences may be destructive to many. In the face of moral ambiguity the struggle for justice proceeds knowing that the present state of affairs is too unacceptable for an humane people. The dilemmas of liberation, the determining of means for ends, of withdrawal for uniting, of destruction for creativity, of identity for unity, of death for new life, are unavoidable in many revolutionary struggles.

Thurman gives such little attention to the contingency that redemptive consequences may not be possible through nonviolence, one must question whether he seriously considers this possible. In his saying, "Unless the actual status of a human being as such is denied, reconciliation between people always has a chance to be effective," there is still the liberal notion of having an option which avoids the compromising of one's highest principles. The contingency of being without redemptive consequences through nonviolence is not hypothetical or infrequent to liberation struggles. With self-righteous injustice and incalcitrant violence as part of the status quo, immediate action is necessary which realistically assesses not only the ideal nature in which the human spirit should act, but the way unjust power yields to power for justice.

Howard Thurman's philosophy of nonviolence is probably influenced by his perceptions of social change *in America*. Though he witnessed injustice and severe castigations of blacks, he could locate within America's founding principles, as manifested in the *Constitution* and *Declaration of Independence*, ideals which declared equality among and the right to justice of all the country's citizens.[75] While the social climate might have been suffocating and deadly, there were national ideals to which one could appeal as the standard for corrective action. If the local municipality was unjust, then state and federal government might intervene. If legislation was unjust, then the judicial system might provide the proper legal sanction for social relations. If the communities of the South were too entrenched in customs of segregation then the appeal could be taken to Northern liberals who recognized the bad image segregation gave the "American way." If all rights were denied, the right to protest injustice remained sacrosanct and flourished in many parts of the nation.

In these "if, then" examples the point is made that within the American political tradition are laws, ideals, and appeal processes which are susceptible to nonviolent protest. Nonviolence can make an impact in this country such that unjust situations begin to feel the pressures of the American conscience.

Nonviolence is a method which is able to make Americans strive to live up to their own book of rules. The chances for its effectiveness may not be guaranteed, the odds may be nine to one against it, the pace of change may be unbearably slow, but the method is viable in this country. Howard Thurman is astute in being one of the first persons to champion its usefulness for minority protest.

If Thurman needed an other-than-America reference to verify his beliefs, he received confirmation in his 1936 visit with Mahatma Gandhi. Thurman talked with the modern master of the method in a country which had millions of people suffering under oppressive rule. The end result of the conversation was that Thurman felt assured that nonviolence could transform whatever difficulties it confronted. The techniques might have to be refined, individuals would need to go through radical preparation to be faithful disciples of the method, large numbers of people might suffer and die, but the moral and spiritual imperatives for nonviolence would prevail over the experiences of violence.[76]

However, this other-than-America experience, as pointed out by Alinsky and Morris, was in a country which honored political principles that made nonviolence an effective mechanism of protest. The morality of nonviolence may be situational and contextual. In some circumstances it may be love abounding, in others it may reflect a naive commitment which has lost its sense of place and timing. Nonviolence as a universal principle for change, as one which can be exported anywhere at anytime, is highly questionable. This issue helps clarify the characterization of Thurman as "an American prophet." His insights, ideals, beliefs, and convictions have been informed by the American experience.

Liberation and Reconciliation

As Thurman's commitments to nonviolence differ from others who focus on the dynamics of revolutionary struggle, his beliefs on reconciliation would be unacceptable among some revolutionaries. The issues of liberation, justice, and power are so central to the dynamic of struggle that reconciliation among revolutionaries means "a needed realignment of power relations" rather than a concept of love which stresses understanding, fellowship, caring, and the elimination of contradictions."

In Maoist and Marxist thought, contradiction is viewed as permanent, absolute, and positive. It is the way revolution overthrows the status quo and continues to remake the social order for the benefit of the masses.

156

"Reconciliation" has been a suspect concept among revolutionaries. Alinsky says the world has consistently used the term to mean "when one side gets the power and the other side gets reconciled to it, then we have reconciliation;. . ."[78]

Thurman's position would be viewed by some theologians as not just poor political analysis or limited personal experience in totalitarian states or idealistic hopes for society, but as bad theology which ignores the liberation motifs of scripture and the Bible's emphasis on the "fallen" state of humanity which has a will to oppressive power. Theological development of these themes is found in Liberation and Black Theology. These kerygmatic theologies often cite biblical passages which describe the exodus of the Hebrews from oppressive Egypt, and the ensuing "holy" wars which had to be fought to preserve this freedom. In Jesus Christ the drama continued with God providing the saving power against the enslavement of sin (personal and social). Even after humanity's rejection, God was able to manifest, through the resurrection, the ability to have final victory over all threats to freedom, even death. The corrupt nature of humanity is clearly evident, and the inevitability of violence is a foregone conclusion. Though reconciliation with God and one's fellows is sought, struggle in the world is absolute, at least until God's intervention builds the Kingdom.

James Cone, the leading proponent of

Black Theology, would consider Thurman's reconciliation emphasis as a concept which ignores the critical process of attaining justice, freedom, and identity. This leads Cone to a different conclusion than Thurman on the morality of violence, a conclusion which closely resembles the Maoist's view previously stated. Cone writes:

> The Christian does not decide between violence and nonviolence, evil and good. He decides between the less and the greater evil. He must ponder whether revolutionary violence is less or more deplorable than the violence perpetuated by the system. There are no absolute rules which can decide the answer with certainty. But he must make a choice. If he decides to take the "nonviolent" way, then he is saying that revolutionary violence is more detrimental to man in the long run than systemic violence. But if the system is evil, then revolutionary violence is both justified and necessary.[79]

This is not to suggest that a serious consideration of struggle and scripture leads to a general acceptance of violence as an appropriate means of change. To the contrary, many advocates of nonviolence are politically astute and biblically oriented. But one can understand how Thurman's disinterest in concentrating on social mechanisms, and his use of religious experience as the primary authority for faith, would make his

158

social change philosophy vulnerable to critics with a different theological commitment.[80] If Thurman had explicated the use of nonviolence within a variety of political contexts, and its justification in light of a biblical witness of violent liberation, he would reinforce his argument prescribing nonviolence as the means for social transformation.

Thurman needed to provide more discourse on the complexities and ambiguities of his social witness concepts. In various writings he cautions that issues of morality are not to be oversimplified, and that legitimate ethical responses are difficult to discern for particular contexts. For example, while arguing for "complete sincerity" in all relations, he recognizes there are questions which make this position difficult. He asks:

> Is there a fine distinction between literal honesty and honesty in spirit and intent? Or is truth telling largely a matter of timing? Are there times when to tell the truth is to be false to the truth that is in you?[81]

The dearth of critical writing in these areas of social witness may best be characterized as a matter of *emphasis*, rather than naivete. This decision of *emphasis* may be explained after one considers Thurman's perceptions of the period in which he lived.

Throughout his writings it is clear that he considered the life of the American black as a precarious existence which was constantly threatened with abuse and death. It is in this context that Thurman sought an answer to the range of issues which confronted the religious and social welfare of blacks. The divide between black and white, victim and perpetrator, oppressed and oppressor was so great, that to speak about justice and social mechanisms for justice seemed like folly. These are only realistic solutions in a situation where power is shared and all parties are considered within the other's ethical field. Thurman, therefore, focused his social witness on creating a *climate for change, a climate for justice*. If the proper conditions were established, then the pursuit of justice and social mechanisms had a possibility for realization.

The creation of this climate of justice would best be grounded in a spiritual transformation of persons—a transformation where people had a proper sense of self and others as God's children—a transformation which recognized the supremacy of love and the fulfillment of community. Unless this spiritual conversion occurred, any social structure of justice, any truce in brutality, was built upon a very tenuous foundation. The counsel of George Cross to address the "timeless hunger of the human spirit" and Rufus Jones's linkage of mysticism to social change are apparent in Thurman's approach.

Howard Thurman's temperament is another important ingredient in understanding his social witness. Thurman confesses that while

160

he loves people and enjoys their fellowship, there is an aspect of his personality which is shy, retreating from any kind of crowd or mass social movement, and not very comfortable with group organizing.[82] His ministry was, therefore, to provide leadership within a defined community which was gathered for spiritual renewal, inter-personal relating, and help in understanding the relationship of self to the social order. He did not attempt to educate and train community members for the sophisticated involvements of power politics.

Likewise, his intellectual energy was primarily given to issues which corresponded with his temperament. The transformation of social structures and development of social mechanisms for justice were important to him, but they did not captivate his interest as the fundamental issues nor as the arenas of thought and action to which he could speak with authority and confidence.

Perhaps Thurman's grounding in mystical experience explains this temperament. Mystical experiences gave him religious knowledge and the sense of loving relationship. The essence of the experience for Thurman is truth, power, and caring. The implication for community is involvement with the structures and systems of society. As a mystic, his *authority* came from being absorbed in experiencing the "essence." He could help others apprehend the significance and complexities of religious experience

161

because it was dominant in shaping his own identity. Familiarity with religious experience gave him *confidence* in public functions (i.e., preaching, lecturing, counselling, administering a religious institution) where the goal was the heightening of awareness through religious experience. His ministry was built upon this strength.

The Value of Models

Persons might criticize Thurman's leadership in the ministry of The Church for the Fellowship of All Peoples if they had an ecclesiology which required the church to participate actively as an *institution* in the social and political issues of society. Thurman's ecclesiology could be characterized as providing a "lemonade stand" for parishioners, where they get refreshed to do personal battle with issues, but the *institution* wields no major power upon structures and forces in society. The church needs to offer its institutional influence not only to encourage individual bodies, but to *become* a body which exercises power in the political decisions effecting community life.

This criticism has merit, but Thurman was not attempting to create the model church for social action involvement. His interest was in developing a model for inclusive religious fellowship. Racial separation was the evil he attacked through building church community. The church as an effective institutional witness in the arena of social action was a different frontier. If Thurman was claiming Fellowship Church to be *the* model of church life, then certainly the model has its shortcomings. But like Thurman, the church made a specific witness which fit its character and mission for its time and place.

The other major critical comment on Thurman's witness could focus on his ministry of establishing models of community. Two questions arise: First, how useful are models which vary from the mainstream of church life? Thurman's campus ministries and his nondenominational church experienced their successes amidst different circumstances than most churches confront. The colleges were controlled educational environments. Fellowship Church did not have to struggle continually with denominational politics. And since it was founded upon inter-racial and inter-cultural principles, it did not have to confront a tradition, history, and people whose experience with that church had been completely contrary to its inclusive tenets.

This is not to suggest that organizing such a church was easy. In many ways, the lack of denominational support or generations of church members complicated the task. But one can make an analogy to Thurman's description of America as a land which was ready for the experiment with democracy because it was not burdened by traditions opposing such innovation. Fellowship Church had an advantage in conducting its experimental community because it was not encumbered by church polity, a history of exclusion, or an ecclesiastical hierarchy which limited its boldness in creating the model. The church did not have the burdensome circumstances in which most churches find themselves.

Fellowship Church may be less relevant as a model for "how to" transform churches into inter-racial and inter-faith communities, and more relevant in providing the witness that such communities are possible and rewarding. The methods and programs for churches which have deep roots in the past may have to differ from Thurman's methods and programs. These churches may not even be able to achieve Fellowship Church's inclusive character in many areas of church life.

While Fellowship Church may not serve as the paradigm for developing the inclusive church, its accomplishments offer a realized alternative to the segregated church. Fellowship Church witnesses to the practice of an ideal. And this actualized vision, this existing community, is an example which churches did not have before Fellowship Church. Such an example is often necessary to encourage and inspire others to test the possibilities within their setting.

The second question concerning Fellowship Church is: How effective are models which are not promoted into ongoing programs? The politics of models is at issue here, such that the model does not become the sole example of an ideal. How does one duplicate the experience in other situations? While pastoring the church, Thurman communicated through lectures, newsletters, and magazine interviews the church's work. After assuming his responsibilities at Boston University he wrote *Footprints of a Dream* which related the beginnings, philosophy, organization, and activities of Fellowship Church. This kind of communication was not, however, mobilizing a structure or movement which could develop one's model into a systematic organization to transform similar institutions. Without some formal organization dedicated to spreading the model or its convictions, there is little chance of having any widespread continued impact on other religious bodies. The church may have missed the opportunity to stimulate change by its failure to become more aggressive in promoting its insights.

Two perspectives which might explain the church's lack of initiative in promotion are: 1) Thurman did not have the missionary or movement temperament, and 2) Thurman was not interested in developing a model that was actively engaged in changing other churches, but was concerned about proving a religious principle of inclusiveness. When the principle was verified the church's primary mission had been accomplished.

The significance of Fellowship Church during its most vital periods of the 1940s and early 1950s is declared by the large

165

numbers of people who supported it, and the many magazine articles relating its work. Its significance during the 1960s, 1970s, 1980s and beyond is uncertain. Fellowship Church's importance to American Christianity is not in being the progenitor of a major denominational or ecclesiastical movement, but in possibilities it demonstrated for inclusive church worship and fellowship.

Thurman's writings, speeches, and ministry identified and responded to serious omissions in theological discourse and church life. In doing this, his own work raises questions which are not adequately addressed by him. Other theologians will have to cover issues and methodological problems which Thurman has omitted from his work. Thurman's achievements, however, still merit his being considered as a major contributor to the "creative edge" of America's religious thought and life. His prophetic witness forcefully answered a crisis of community with imagination and effectiveness.

Chapter V

THE AUTHORITY WITHIN

The mystic depends upon religious experience to disclose truth. Insights from the
experience are utilized for interpreting life.
But mystical experience is not the only
source of a mystic's theology. The mystic
perceives his/her own life as a source of
revelation. Since the Ultimate dwells within
finite experience, one's own existence
contains revelations about reality and the
will of God. Sensitive examination of one's
life can yield wisdom. The theology of
mystics, therefore, is often autobiographical.
Howard Thurman's theology is also con-
ceived on this method. In speaking and
writing, his ideas are grounded in personal
experiences.

In a meditation entitled "The Inward Sea"
Thurman writes:

> There is in every person an inward
> sea, and in that sea is an island and
> on that island there is an altar and
> standing guard before that altar is the
> "angel with the flaming sword." Noth-
> ing can get by that angel to be
> placed upon that altar unless it has

> the mark of your inner authority.
> Nothing passes "the angel with the
> flaming sword" to be placed upon
> your altar unless it be a part of "the
> fluid area of your consent." This is
> your crucial link with the Eternal.[1]

Previous chapters have tied Thurman's intellectual development to the influence of pivotal mentors. The exchanges between teachers and student have been identified as crucial contexts which nurtured his religious thinking. But why did his "angel with the flaming sword" permit their gifts to be placed upon his "altar"? The answer may reside in pivotal life experiences which tutored the angel—experiences that revealed how one's self is blessed or desecrated—that which nurtures or violates the personality—that which adorns or vandalizes the altar. His life experiences help in explaining how his theology evolved.

The Wisdom of Experience

Early Crises

The experiential bases for Thurman's liberal theology are possibly discovered by analyzing crucial events in the formative years of his childhood. Several encounters with the church resulted in his developing a highly critical posture on the church's authority and role.

Thurman's father (Saul Thurman) was not

a member of a church. Thurman recalls that his father felt he would "lose his soul" by making such an affiliation.[2] At Saul Thurman's funeral the preacher considered this lack of church membership as evidence that Saul Thurman's soul was condemned to hell, and therefore berated him before the community as "an object lesson to all unbelievers, to all sinners." This traumatic experience so embittered seven year old Howard Thurman that he said: "When I grow up to be a man, one thing is sure, I'll never have anything to do with the church."[3]

Later, however, at age twelve Thurman felt that his religious experience required him to join the church. He went before the Deacons and gave his reasons for seeking membership. The Deacons considered his explanation inadequate and sent him home. Only through the intervention of his grandmother did they reconsider and agree to accept him.

During these early years of his life he continued to have personal, intense, and highly disturbing encounters with the church's authority figures. In these instances, as the church carried out its functions, Thurman felt its insensitivity and the violence of its dogma. He would always be aware of its frailty—of its fallibility as a truth bearer, of its shortcomings in verifying religious experience—frailties which emphasized an ethos of exclusion, be it excluding one from heaven (his father) or one from

169

church membership (himself).

This excluding nature of many churches particularly affected Thurman when he realized how racial separatism was deeply embedded in church life. During his seminary years his white roommates were chastised by the school's administration for breaking tradition in deciding to room with a black person (Thurman). And because he was black, Thurman was asked to withdraw as a pallbearer at the funeral for the seminary's white maintenance man.[4] This church institution appeared to acquiesce to social mores rather than provide a challenging religious witness for inclusiveness. In these experiences the institutional church had demonstrated to Thurman its susceptibility to sin, prejudice, fear, and other destructive forces which emanate from society.

Consistent with the liberal tradition, Thurman had little use for the symbols and rituals of the institutional church. This attitude can also be associated with events in his childhood. When confronted by students at Boston University (while he was Dean of the chapel), who were concerned about his removing a brass cross from the chapel's altar, he replied by telling them that the cross invariably reminded him of the Ku Klux Klan burning a cross at the end of his street. He concluded by saying: "And I'm not going to have my Sundays spoiled by the imagery which that thing burned into my adolescent heart."[5]

Thurman's thinking on symbols, rituals,

and dogma was also influenced when he was a youth employed by an Episcopal church. His responsibilities were to pump the hand-pumped church organ for the organist to practice and conduct choir rehearsal. He was never allowed to do this on Sunday, for then he would have to be in full view of the white congregation during worship. This practice of the church deadened any interest of his in their extensive use of symbolism, dogma, and rituals; for surely these could not carry much meaning if the church did not include him as a full member of the religious family.'

This exclusion caused Thurman to distrust ceremony, doctrine, and symbols as truth bearers. In his thinking they were inventions of the mind to manifest a deeper meaning. Consequently, they were subject to any self-serving purpose which the mind could devise. These types of personal encounters with the institutional church revealed for Thurman the social sources of church traditions—sources too conditioned by human limitations to interpret adequately or give expression to the religious experience he had come to know.

Accompanying Thurman's critical perspective on church life is a deep love and loyalty for the church—a love for the church's founding principles of community building, and a loyalty to its potential to actualize its claims as a faithful instrument of God. This love and loyalty were also nurtured during childhood. Thurman's mother and grandmother kept him active in their local church, and they enabled him to develop respect, appreciation, and commitment for the church. Their love and loyalty for the church prevented him from condemning the church by his negative experiences.[7]

The necessity to distinguish particular problems from the essential nature of the church was made by Thurman's grandmother when someone reported to her that persons had caused such turmoil at their local church that some members were planning to leave it. Her response to the situation was: "If a rattlesnake got into my house. . .I'd put the snake out, not move myself."[8]

Nancy Ambrose was a significant influence, not just for her intellect, but because of the power and authority she exercised in his life. She became for Thurman a source of protection, hope, and faith. His self felt grounded in her. Elizabeth Yates, Thurman's biographer, describes Nancy Ambrose's significance to him as follows:

> She backed up her word with action and he knew he could count on her. He boasted to his friends of her, saying she could kill a bear with her fist. No one disputed him, though no one felt a need for a test. There was not a person in the Negro community on the shore of the Halifax River who had not at a time of trouble felt anchored by her strength. She was a haven to them all.

> More than anyone else, she made
> Howard feel his significance, not only
> as a Negro boy but as a Child of
> God.[9]

Throughout his lectures and writings, Thurman speaks of his grandmother in saintly, yet intimate tones.

The prominence he gives to her ideas and example can be understood when one considers her meaning in the making of his personality. In a period of Thurman's life when his world seemed wrought with insecurity and death, she had attributes which translated into power. She acted as one who had inner authority. Rather than being controlled by her environment she exercised control over it. Nancy Ambrose became a role model for him. She was the *exemplary* mentor.

It is not difficult to see her influence in Thurman's stress that the individual, rather than the institution or the group, is the key to social change. She was an individual who survived personal tragedy, challenged the church, influenced the local community, found integrity and worth in her racial identity, fearlessly confronted any aggressive action from their hostile environment, and who drew upon personal religious experience as the source for her life. In surmising she had a proper sense of self, Thurman could then perceive how this kind of individual became the basis for creatively making the loving community.

More than institutions, organizations, or systems of thought, she made a difference to his world. She revealed the power of love as a more compelling force than hate. She was the embodiment of the theological principles which shaped Thurman's thought on the individual, religion, and social change. Nancy Ambrose was not just the bearer of ideas and concepts for Thurman. She was the bearer of experience itself.

Early Mysticism

Thurman's earliest contact with mysticism was through mystical experiences, and not in learning a system of thought about it. In recalling moments of highest meaning during his youth, he mentions mystical experiences with nature. His nature mysticism included the Halifax River which triggered a "Presence that spoke to him without a voice, revealed itself to him without a vision." It included an oak tree to which he talked over all his troubles.[10] It included all of nature which gave him a sense of unity and identity:

> As a boy in Florida, I [Thurman] walked along the beach of the Atlantic in the quiet stillness that can only be completely felt when the murmur of the ocean is stilled and the tides move stealthily along the shore. I held my breath against the night and watched the stars etch their brightness on the face of the darkened

174

canopy of the heavens. I had the sense that all things, the sand, the sea, the stars, the night, and I were *one* lung through which all of life breathed. Not only was I aware of a vast rhythm enveloping all, but I was a part of it and it was a part of me.[11]

These mystical experiences effected by nature met Howard Thurman's most basic needs for emotional survival. His whole person depended upon the self-meaning received during these times.

These experiences were necessary because Thurman felt dehumanized and threatened by much of his social environment. He writes:

I was a very sensitive child who suffered much from the violences of racial conflict. The climate of our town, Daytona Beach, Florida, was better than most Southern towns because of the influence of the tourists who wintered there. Nevertheless, life became more and more suffocating because of the fear of being brutalized, beaten, or otherwise outraged. In my effort to keep this fear from corroding my life and making me seek relief in shiftlessness, I sought help from God. I found that the more I turned to prayer, to what I discovered in later years to be meditation, the more time I spent alone in the woods or on the beach, the freer became my own spirit and the more realistic became my ambitions to get an education.[12]

Mysticism was a resource of meaning when political power, social protest, legal rights, Christian ethics, and church influence appeared powerless to protect him. *Alone* in nature he found a primary context for his "proper sense of self."

This biographical insight yields further understanding on Thurman's theological positions. His first principle that a person should believe in him or her self is an outgrowth of his mysticism. He is convinced that the individual can withstand and creatively effect any hostile force. His experiences of ultimate meaning lead him to conclude that the individual is the key to community because the individual is the direct recipient of divine meaning and power. Thurman's feeling of being cared for and loved in these experiences can account for his development of the love-ethic as the basis for Christianity.

Perhaps his interpretation of the ministry of Jesus can be credited to his beliefs about mysticism and the individual: that Jesus who also experienced a nonsupportive social environment must have drawn upon mystical experiences to emerge as the powerful individual to lead a people from the oppression of the Roman Empire.[13] Young Thurman's talks with Jesus as a *friend* could have led him to know that Jesus truly did care for the disinherited because Jesus cared about his problems.

In addition to this high assessment on the worth of the individual, Thurman's mysticism provided the basis for his vision of community. In these experiences he felt a Presence, a oneness, a unity despite the segregation and alienation found in the life of Daytona, Florida. He knew a reality of wholeness in the midst of realities of fragmentation. His inner reality became the vision and experience which he longed to see and feel in his locality.

The encounter with the divine became the key to realizing the ultimate purpose of social relationships. So when Thurman expresses his convictions about the possibility for community he is not just theorizing, but speaking from a personal experience of community which he believes can be duplicated in the social order.

In adulthood, Thurman develops the concept that "the contradictions of life are not final." This leads to the corollary that the dissonance of the social order must eventually yield to the more compelling urge for unity found in religious experience—an urge which proved itself during his youth.

Howard Thurman's reliance upon mysticism may have effected his temperament as a participant in social change. Society, institutions, and organizations did not provide the meaning he received from personal religious experience. Thurman's worth was often denied or belittled by the social order. He attributes his proper sense of self to an intensely personal process:

> I have never been in search of iden-
> tity—and I think the explanation is
> that everything I've ever felt and
> worked on and believed in was
> founded in a kind of private, almost
> unconscious autonomy that did not
> seek vindication in my environment
> because it was in me.[14]

Consequently, as Thurman did not depend on groups for identity, neither did he feel very comfortable participating in social protest (i.e., rallies, picketing, demonstrations) which aimed at forming a proper social context for a proper sense of self. They were not part of his background, nor were they primary in shaping his personality. He felt ill at ease at these events. This uneasiness might account for his theological and ministry emphases on spiritual processes, rather than the processes of social mechanisms.

Thurman's attitude can be interpreted as a desire to maintain *control* over his life—to feel completely responsible for personal integrity and actions. Mystical experience provided an arena where other persons or structures had no final authority or power. It established boundaries in which he was sure of all the parties (he and God) involved in the experience. In living the spiritual life he did not have to present his decisions to a committee, or "politic" for a vote, or make forced compromises and concessions.

This notion of personal control is highly valued by Thurman. In a lecture entitled "Mysticism and Jesus," he relates the greatness of Jesus to the ability to focus his life around the new self awareness gained from the mystical experience of baptism, rather than depending on the Jewish community's expectations for him. And Thurman interprets Jesus' refusal to enter political activity as a decision which recognized that demands and expectations would be placed upon him which would hinder his ministry to the spiritual crises of his people.[15]

Thurman expresses the belief that social activism makes time, energy, and moral demands which can lessen the control a person has over his or her commitments. It can take away one's initiative over life. This is not to imply that social activism is an illegitimate response of faithfulness and commitment to God. For some people it may be the best expression of their abilities. They may be so skilled at their activism that there is no loss of personal initiative. Or the significance of their labor may make them willing to sacrifice initiative. But for others like Thurman, the price to be paid for such involvement too drastically effects the commitment to their primary religious calling in life.

Thurman felt his calling to "the hunger of the spirit" would be damaged by responsibilities of social activism. He was not opting for a quietistic faith, for he accepted the trauma, frustration, hostility, and difficulties which accompany a ministry to improving interpersonal relations and establishing a creative church witness which challenged social traditions and customs. His commitment for social transformation encouraged the activism of others, but recognized his limitations as a technician of social mechanisms.

His temperament defined his role as theologian and minister. This role articulated creative religious understandings and models of ministry for social change, even understandings which are useful principles for social activism.

Thurman professes that periods of withdrawal from social action are not just a preference of one's personality, but necessary for making worthwhile contributions to the social order. Personal religious experience is essential to creative social transformation. In his books, *The Inward Journey* and *Meditations of the Heart,* Thurman writes meditations which express the exigency for individual reflection and self-examination which lead to a profound resolve for a higher quality of life. The reflecting and examining require one to experience isolation from the normal pattern of events. Such meditations as "Silence is a Door to God," "An Island of Peace Within One's Soul," "A Lull in the Rhythm of Doing," and "In the Moment of Pause, the Vision of

God," stress that certain purposes and meanings are only revealed when the individual has the setting of isolation. Then and only then is the self encounter and the God-person encounter possible.[16]

Thurman perceives isolation not as an artificial environment which removes one from reality, but it allows true individual reality to be manifest. And when one discovers individual reality, one has the key to discovering universal reality. In *Deep Is the Hunger* he writes:

> It is the solitariness of life that makes it move with such ruggedness. All life is one, and yet life moves in such intimate circles of awful individuality. The power of life perhaps is its aloneness. . . . Each soul must learn to stand up in its own right and live. . . Ultimately, I am alone, so vastly alone that in my aloneness is all the life of the universe. Stripped to the life literal substance of myself, there is nothing left but naked soul, the irreducible ground of individual being, which becomes at once the quickening throb of God. At such moments of profound awareness I seem to be all that there is in the world, and all that there is in the world seems to be myself.[17]

This isolation which results in the feeling of "loneliness" or "aloneness" is the context for insightful, creative, and committed living.

After noting that loneliness can be the result of fear, bitterness, death, and despair, Thurman says:

> But there is loneliness in another key. There is the loneliness of the truth-seeker whose search swings him out beyond all frontiers and all boundaries until there bursts upon his view a fleeting moment of utter awareness and he *knows* beyond all doubt, all contradictions. There is the loneliness of the moment of integrity when the declaration of the self is demanded and the commitment gives no corner to sham, to pretense, or to lying. There is the loneliness in the moment of creation when the new comes into being, trembles, then steadies and finds its way. There is the loneliness of those who walk with God until the path takes them out beyond all creeds and all faiths and they know the wholeness of communion, and the bliss of finally being understood.[18]

In recalling his decision to leave Howard University and work with Fellowship Church, Thurman tells of the lack of support he received from persons who failed to grasp his vision of the significance of the new venture.[19] He explains this consequence by saying "the way of the pioneer is a lonely journey."[20]

His own ministry bears witness to the innovative results which grew because of an independence from social and political activism. Here again the personal, alone-with-nature experiences of his youth can be understood as the informing experiences for his ideas about solitude.

It is possible to conclude that Thurman's reluctance to lead socio-political organizations and to join protest movements can be attributed to a personality which found primary nurture, identity, and meaning in private experiences. His witness also leads to another conclusion; that is, the private life provided Thurman a sense of understanding about and mission to social mechanisms and structures. He developed an acute awareness of the underlying spiritual issues which determine the creative or destructive direction of social organisms, and from this awareness dedicated himself to a ministry of building models of community and to helping persons who are involved with socio-political organizations.

Aloneness is not just a preference of personality but at times a sacrifice for faithful witness. It is not an escape from social organizations but a preparation to address them significantly.

Self-Actualization

Thurman's ideas are shaped by life experiences and his interpretation of them. Continuing with this focus can yield more than just a greater understanding about the making of his *thought*, it can also help in understanding the *person* of Thurman—not just what he thinks, but who he is.

This concern is especially important since Thurman is often acknowledged as a charismatic figure who intensely affected and motivated people with the power of his personality.[21] Discerning and assessing those qualities of personality which explain charisma and creativity is difficult. They are often the result of some rare combination of timing, social temperament, and circumstance. One cannot program an individual to be charismatic or creative, for they are inherent qualities which are not taught, but nurtured.

A very useful article which attempts to discover the primary characteristics of creative leadership is Frederick D. Harper's "Self-Actualization and Three Black Protesters."[22] Harper utilizes Abraham Maslow's theory on self-actualization as the basis for understanding the personalities of Frederick Douglass, Malcolm X, and Martin Luther King, Jr. In Harper's and Maslow's work is the conclusion that outstanding creative historical figures can be identified as self-actualized persons.

Self-actualization as described by Maslow is:

> . . . the full use and exploitation of talents, capacities, potentialities, etc. Such people seem to be fulfilling

> themselves and to be doing the best
> that they are capable of doing, re-
> minding us of Nietzsche's exhortation,
> "Become what thou art!" They are
> people who have developed or are
> developing to the full stature of
> which they are capable.[23]

Self-actualized people are lifted up in culture as those who represent the best in psychological health. They become models of potential and constructive living. They so influence and affect others that their lives are often considered exemplary.

Using Maslow's fifteen categories of actualization, characteristics can be identified within Howard Thurman which account for his personal power and social appeal. Maslow's categories are: 1) a more efficient perception of reality and more comfortable relations with it, 2) acceptance of the basic integrity of self and others, 3) spontaneity, 4) a sense of mission or problem centeredness, 5) detachment, 6) autonomy, 7) a deep appreciation of "the basic goods of life," 8) mystical experience, 9) identification with humankind, 10) "deeper and more profound relations than any other adults," 11) a democratic character structure, 12) discrimination between means and ends, 13) an unhostile sense of humor, 14) crea-tiveness, and 15) resistance to encultura-tion.[24]

In relating Thurman's personality traits to Maslow's characteristics it becomes clear that Thurman consistently matches the descriptions of a self-actualized person.[25] This is particularly interesting when considering the emphasis Thurman puts on realizing one's potential. He accomplished ("accomplished" does not mean a completed process of growth, but to be fully involved in the process) the basic principle which he considered as the purpose of the individual.

Identifying Thurman as a self-actualized person does not imply that he was perfect. Perfection is not a concern of self-actualization. Actualization is the process of fully utilizing one's abilities and potential. While self-actualizers are not perfect, they are extraordinary for they represent the best in the development of human personality. It is estimated that "a fraction of one percent" of the population merits such a unique status.[26] Consequently, they command the respect and admiration of others who are seeking models of psychological health and fulfillment in living. This may provide an answer in explaining Thurman's charisma.

As stated, one can find aspects of Thurman's personality which match all of Maslow's criteria. The category which particularly shaped Thurman's life was "mystical experience." Mystical experience provided the vision of reality and self-actualization. Its feelings of assurance freed Thurman to have a quality of detachment and autonomy. His response to the experience led him into a creative ministry based on problem-centeredness and identification with humanity. It was in response to mystic feeling that other traits of his personality developed. Self-actualization was the result of his response to religious experience.

Mysticism was at the heart of Thurman's theological and personal identity. The experiences enabled him to discover his true status before God and his relation to creation. It was not necessary for outside sources to define this for him. He came to rely upon his abilities to find meaning and assurance in his religious experiences. This gave Thurman confidence in himself. George Cross helped Thurman trust the insights of his (Thurman's) personality in religious inquiry; but this was an external confirmation and cultivation of what Thurman had done intuitively since childhood.

Thurman understood the processes of his life as providing empirical evidence of certain verities of existence. When I was with Thurman while he listened to tapes of his meditations and sermons, I could see that he was deeply affected by his messages. His facial expressions and body posture were animated responses to what he was hearing. Thurman was inspired, convicted, and taught by the truth which came through him. His own life served as a fundamental authority for wisdom and faith.

So in accounting for Thurman's religious liberalism, one is not only drawn to pivotal mentors, but to pivotal life experiences as the primary context from which to gain a critical perspective on religion and on doing theology. The actualization of the self is a process which reveals and affirms the authority within.

Deep Calls Unto Deep

Thurman's large following is best understood by focusing on his personality, and not just his ideas. His charisma is the result of persons feeling related to him. Certainly his religious concepts have attracted adherents, but persons primarily speak about a sense of relationship with him.

Paul Chaffee, in an unpublished essay entitled "The Spiritual Ground of Pastoral Theology: The Life and Thought of Howard Thurman," explicates the basis of this rapport by describing Thurman as one of the outstanding pastoral theologians. Pastoral theology has an "inclusive and caring point of view." Chaffee further defines this term:

> For Thurman it means first and foremost an extraordinary care for his audience, the auditor or reader. This extends naturally to counseling activities in a direct way. The care can be seen in *how* he uses word and thoughts. In both writing and speaking, he has taken generalization, with all its attendant dangers, and made it a fine art. It succeeds because it strives to plow the common ground of every individual's experience at such a deep level that to participate in the dialogue, even as listeners, creates a distinct impression of intimacy. He identifies what is personally

recognizable in such an imaginative and probing fashion that we are given back to ourselves renewed.[27]

The experience of caring was communicated in Thurman's preaching style. He did not promote his ideas and win a following by haranguing individuals about their lifestyles, and advocating the need for them to follow his prescription for salvation. His method was to share his vision and hope that whatever truth he proclaimed was accepted by others in a "contagious" way, so that persons might sense a more compelling verity which defines and transforms their lives.[28]

Thurman communicated what he considered to be the essence of religion. He was not interested in persuading people to believe certain doctrines, dogma, theological systems, creeds or way of doing biblical interpretation. He did not publicly belittle orthodoxy or its adherents. He focused on the dimension of faith which heightens one's sense of self, community, and God. It was possible for his hearers to remain orthodox in their beliefs and be inspired by Thurman without feeling any contradiction. In speaking to the *essence* of Christianity he spoke, as George Cross taught, to the *essence* of orthodoxy.

This style of ministry is itself a witness to the possibilities for community in the midst of diversity. Though Thurman is an exponent of modernistic liberalism, he does

189

not attempt to convert persons to this theology. Though orthodoxy is not part of his thinking, he does not have the reputation as an antagonist to the orthodox position. Thurman is not perceived as an attacker against whom the defenses must be raised. Persons feel that the essence of their faith is affirmed, accompanied by a vision to realize their potential. These feelings of affirmation and caring have given Thurman a very broad and diverse constituency which receives him and his ideas with enthusiasm.

The sensation of intimacy is not only because Thurman addresses the concerns of others, but also because he lays bare his inner life. In speaking and writing he discloses the struggles, pain, humor, embarrassments, despair, and hope of his life. The listener or reader feels entrusted with a viewing of Thurman's self. He allows his audience to know how he has wrestled with God and the hard questions of life, and how this process has not only brought answers and resolution, but more questions and tension.

The naked exposure to someone's self is a privilege reserved for intimate relationships. It involves trust on the part of the giver, and assumes care from the receiver. The willingness to share one's self is an invitation to intimacy—an intimacy that invites one to the holy ground of the heart (the indwelling abode of God), creating the opportunity for the listener to encounter the Divine and have his/her own religious experience.

I have heard many testimonies of persons who profess that hearing Thurman ushered them to a profound experience of God. Thurman's oratory is the primary vehicle for this occurrence. Truly, in Thurman, "the medium is the message." The emotional dimensions of the subject under discussion are transmitted through an emotional Thurman whose voice inflection, long pauses, facial expressions, and gestures convey that he, at the moment of speaking, feels the emotion. Thurman seems to speak from the center of his being. One "listens in" on the immediate experience of Thurman engaging ideas, feelings, and God. The audience is not witnessing a perform-ance, a rehearsed act where the speaker is more "role" than "self." The audience is there with Thurman as he, completely absorbed in a thought that permeates his being and effects his appearance, explores the meaning of life.

A variety of sources attest to Thurman's abilities and influence. In his book, *The Oratory of Negro Leaders,* Marcus Boulware describes the appeal of outstanding Negro leaders by saying: "It has become a Prover-bial expression that those who have not heard [Mordecai] Johnson speak, or Howard Thurman preach, or Marian Anderson sing, are not qualified to appear in genteel company."[29]

Thurman's appeal across racial lines is sub-stantiated in two surveys. His popularity among blacks was confirmed in a poll conducted by Ebony magazine in 1954. After "questioning a cross section of churchgoers—including doctors, housewives, laborers, lawyers and teachers," he was selected as one of the ten greatest Negro preachers in America.[30] In 1953 *Life* magazine listed him as one of the twelve greatest preachers in the United States. Thurman was the only black person on a list "determined by a polling of ministers, priests and theological schools of all faiths."[31]

This popularity is related to Thurman's skill and power as a speaker to affect the listener strongly. Boulware provides an impression of this effect:

> In listening to Dr. Thurman preach, the author [Boulware] was lifted spellbound to an apex of spiritual grandeur that often placed him under an enchantment completely separated from the reality of national issues. When under the spell of the man's oratory, a listener can hardly imagine an equal.[32]

Yates, rather than offering a personal reaction, relates the comments of others who have just heard Thurman speak:

> . . . "I feel as if I'd been with Jesus." A white man holds out his hand to help an elderly Negro woman down the steps. "We were there," a girl says, moving quickly through the crowd as if under some

192

urgency to do what she had seen could be done with an aroused imagination. A man with an unmistakable Southern accent speaks to no one in particular "He finds his way into everyone's heart." A woman replies, "He stands aside and lets it happen to you." "His words seemed to be coming from God." "A tremendous spirit has expressed itself in words that we can all understand."[33]

Howard Thurman's speaking not only conveys religious ideas, but his personality reveals the vitality of the ideas—how these ideas effect a life (his own). James McClendon's *Biography as Theology* asserts that exposure to a person's life can give insight into the belief structures that support the moral vision of the community. Biography is theology.[34]

Thurman's life is exemplary of his convictions. One is aware that in him "the word becomes flesh." He is what he expounds. This genuineness between word and person means convictions are not apparel to be worn or discarded at one's pleasure. Convictions are not manifest only when they are acceptable to others. This genuineness means convictions are integral to one's very being. They are manifest in all one does, and are not dependent upon social expectation.

Thurman's career testifies to his commitment to realize his convictions in all he did. His worship services, innovative church, preaching style, writings, Educational Trust, and counseling are consistent expressions of his beliefs. Even in the midst of misunderstanding and ridicule he persevered with his commitment.

This quality indicates the potency of the prophet's authority. When others see how meaning flows through the prophet's life, something within their lives is aroused to discover their source for greater meaning and potential. The prophet is not just an example, but an inspirer; not just a leader, but a maker of leaders; not the authority, but a revealer of authority. Howard Thurman fulfilled such a role by the function and integrity of his being.

Chapter VI

PROPHETIC MYSTICISM

Spirituality and Community

The Prophetic Tradition

Howard Thurman's reliance upon religious experience, as the source of prophetic activity, was a characteristic he held in common with the Hebrew prophets. Religious experience made the prophets aware of God's claim upon them and their role in transforming the community.

Abraham Heschel in his book, *The Prophets*, concludes that the consciousness of Israel's prophets was shaped by intense encounters with God. He writes:

> An analysis of prophetic utterances shows that the fundamental experience of the prophet is a fellowship with the feelings of God, *a sympathy with the divine pathos*, a communion with the divine consciousness which comes about through the prophet's reflection of, or participation in, the divine pathos. The typical prophetic state of mind is one of being taken

up into the heart of the divine pa-
thos.[1]

Heschel continues by asserting that the
purpose of the encounter was to awaken
the prophet to God's concern for right
relationship with the people. The meaning
of religious experience was more social than
personal. The prophet's message was indict-
ing, but also hopeful; it communicated
God's passion for the welfare of God's
people.[2]

Walter Brueggemann's *The Prophetic Imagination* is another helpful source for
understanding the prophetic quality of
Thurman's ministry. Brueggemann develops a
concept of prophecy based upon the tradition of biblical prophets, the life of Jesus,
and the mission of the church.

Four characteristics emerge as indicators of
prophetic ministry: 1) the establishment of
an "alternative community" which is conscious of its unique identity and mission to
others; 2) the prophetic insights are
communicated in every activity of ministry,
and they define sources of life and death
for every context; 3) persons are helped in
seeing the world as it really is, and to
become fully sensitive to the hurt and pain
experienced in life; and 4) "prophetic
ministry seeks to penetrate despair so that
new futures can be believed in and
embraced by us."[3] These characteristics
provide an interpretation of prophetic
functions that are also relevant to modern

times. Thurman's ministry can be correlated with the four expressions of the prophetic. His life provides a modern case study of the nexus between religious experience, prophetic response, and social transformation.

Because Thurman's death is relatively recent, all the "returns" may not be in regarding his contributions to society. The validity of certain concepts and labors may need considerable time to emerge. The revelation of certain truths may require a social, political, and intellectual milieu that resides in the future. Cognizance of the time factor is expressed by Reinhold Niebuhr when he says:

> Nothing that is worth doing can be achieved in a lifetime; therefore, we must be saved by hope. Nothing which is true or beautiful or good makes complete sense in any immediate context of history; therefore we must be saved by faith.[4]

With an eye toward the future, this concluding discussion suggests the enduring importance of Howard Thurman's contributions.

Hearts and Systems

In designating contemporary prophets, a major debate centers on the prophet's role in transforming systems of injustice. It is not just the question of whether the prophet had any influence in causing change, but whether he/she was on the "front lines" of conflict. To some, prophetic activity is, by definition, the organizing of people to assault oppressive structures. This attitude is evident in Benita Eisler's scathing review of Thurman's autobiography, *With Head and Heart*. She finds little that is noteworthy about Thurman's social significance. After listing major social issues of the 1960s she comments:

> Not since the Abolitionist movement had so many American clergymen moved down from their pulpits and into the trenches of social protest and reform. One wants to know, quite simply, why Thurman felt so little impulse to join them.[5]

Such a myopic understanding of prophetic leadership neglects crucial efforts that are integral to liberation. It fails to recognize the hunger for meaning which is not satisfied by political ideology and campaigns—a hunger which must be addressed if persons are to have the commitment and strength to participate in the arduous tasks of structural change.

In addition to his pioneering work on a theology for the disinherited, Thurman's emphasis upon personal spiritual renewal is a crucial contribution to the liberating process. Liberation is not just a change in political and economic institutions, the legal system, or social customs. For liberation to emanate from the oppressed, there must be a change in their response-ability against the oppressive factors. This response-ability is largely an internal transformation where the oppressed realize a new status which redefines their worth and power. They come to attain a proper sense of self.

Liberation theologian Rosemary Ruether recognizes the necessity for this "inward liberation" as a prerequisite for social transformation. She notes how the oppressed, because of an inadequate self image, tend to turn on themselves rather than the power structures. The liberating process of the oppressed must therefore be experienced as "a veritable resurrection of the self."[6]

Martin Luther King, Jr. was also aware that spiritual transformation was necessary for lasting social change. Speaking primarily about the oppressors, he says:

> The ultimate solution to the race problem lies in the willingness of men to obey the unenforceable. . . . Desegregation will break down the legal barriers and bring men together physically, but something must touch the hearts and souls of men so that they will come together spiritually because it is natural and right.[7]

Concentration on this concern is the labor of what Segundo Galilea calls "the prophetic pastoral option." It is the proclamation of a message that arouses a "critical consciousness" that "is capable of inspiring the deepest and most decisive liberating transformations."

The contention that Thurman has affected American life through his impact upon individuals becomes more evident after reflecting on the size of Thurman's audience over the fifty years of his ministry. Jan Corbett, in her article "Howard Thurman: A Theologian for Our Time," describes Thurman as "a person to whose door a fair sample of the world's population is beating a well-worn path."[8] It is difficult to measure, but the probabilities are high that since he is considered by many as their mentor, his thought has influenced their work and relationships in some significant way.[9]

Leaders of social change organizations testify to Thurman's effect upon their lives and work. Whitney M. Young, Jr., the late Executive Director of the National Urban League, Inc., and Roy Wilkins, the late Executive Director of the National Association for the Advancement of Colored People, praised Thurman as an interpreter of the racial problem in America, and as one who creatively articulates a "basis for hope."[10] Vernon Jordan, former President of the National Urban League, indicated that conversations with Thurman and listening to tapes of Thurman's meditations had therapeutic meaning for him as he was recovering from a sniper's attack. He feels Thurman provides society a "vision of God's world." And Jordan believes Thurman will continue to affect lives "so long as men treasure truth, justice, and compassion, friendship."[11]

James Farmer founded the Committee of Racial Equality (C.O.R.E.) in 1942 to fight discrimination and segregation utilizing nonviolent methods. From the mid 1950s through the 1960s C.O.R.E. (the "C" now standing for "Congress") exerted significant national influence for civil rights. James Farmer became C.O.R.E.'s National Director and coordinated its Freedom Rides of the early 1960s. C.O.R.E.'s efforts, under Farmer's leadership, played a major role in achieving the civil rights successes of this period. In a recent conversation with me, Farmer stated that Howard Thurman taught him social ethics at Howard University. And Farmer credits Thurman as the one who planted in him the conviction that Gandhi's nonviolent methods could effect social change in America.

Author and activist, Vincent Harding, recalls that Thurman's *Jesus and the Disinherited* was used by leaders in the civil rights movement as a theological foundation for their activism. They would regularly study and discuss the book together. It provided crucial instruction on nonviolence and the love-ethic as Christian means for overcoming social oppression. The leaders could better understand how to define and maintain their religious identity in the midst of political struggles. Harding believes that this text defined the spiritual issues for social transformation, and that it inspired and emboldened leaders as they engaged in the struggle for justice.[12]

Rev. Jesse Jackson, former President of Operation PUSH, and now heading The Rainbow Coalition is perhaps the nation's leading civil rights activist. Respect for his leadership is verified in surveys aimed at determining the most effective and admired black leader in the United States. *Ebony* magazine reports: "Last year [1980] alone the activist minister led three major polls. . . ."[13] Jackson gives personal testimony to Thurman's influence upon him in saying: "As an activist I was attracted to Dr. Thurman." He believes Thurman "sowed the seeds that bred a generation of activists." Jesse Jackson cherishes Thurman's emphasis on the spiritual dimensions of social change. It is his conviction that Howard Thurman, Benjamin Mays, and Mordecai Johnson "blew away the philosophical underpinnings of racism and segregation." And he suggests that Thurman's capacity to lead one to the deepest issues of social change drew persons like Martin Luther King, Jr., Whitney Young, Otis Moss, and Samuel Procter, who "sat at his [Thurman's] feet."[14]

Otis Moss, noted civil rights activist, offers his witness in saying:

> It might be that he [Thurman] did not join the march from Selma to Montgomery, or many of the other

202

> marches, but he has participated at
> the level that shapes the philosophy
> that creates the march—and without
> that people don't know what to do
> before the march, while they march
> or after they march.[15]

Howard Thurman's prophetic ministry has affected hearts and systems. The personal approach has social implications. His thought and integrity of being have been a source of authority, insight, strength, and inspiration for technicians of social transformation.

Living Water

Harold E. Quinley's *The Prophetic Clergy* is a study of variables that influence the social activism of Protestant ministers. Quinley notes the tension experienced in situations where ministers want to resolve pressing social problems, but laity are more concerned about spiritual revival.[16] This tension often leads to polarization. Ministers are required to make an either/or decision—to choose between either social issues or spiritual matters as the agenda of ministry.

Howard Thurman's thought is a refreshing response to these concerns—a response which makes them a correlation rather than a dichotomy. The quest of the spirit within life's social realities is his hermeneutical gauge for explicating the correlation. This grounding in contextual spirituality should prove ever relevant to America's religious future. One reason for this prediction centers on the perpetual resurgence of piety in the religious life of a people—a piety which reacts to orthodoxy, formality and authority in religion, scientific explanations to the ultimate questions of life, and increased technology and mechanization in the social order.

Alan Watts asserts that modern Western culture has matured to the point where continued advancement now depends upon concerted nurturing in matters of spirituality.[17] The need is so pronounced that Watts terms the present age "the epoch of the Spirit," an epoch characterized by the necessity of mystical religion.[18] Thurman's mysticism addresses the demands of a spirit epoch. The basic identity of his ministry and theology is rooted in Christian spirituality. Over and over Thurman is attempting to answer the question: how does the spirit of God find expression in human experience? Alan Watts calls this interest a theology of the Holy Spirit: "Mystical religion, however, is the special province of the Holy Spirit, and in a certain sense the God of the mystics is the Holy Spirit . . ."[19]

Thurman's focus on the Holy Spirit raises the question of identity within the context of Christian spirituality. As long as piety and spirituality inform the religious journey, Thurman's thought should prevail as a seminal and creative interpretation and response on the life of the spirit.

The other reason for the prediction of

Thurman's continued relevance centers on an ethical necessity for the social order. Rodney Stark and Charles Y. Glock in their book, *American Piety: The Nature of Religious Commitment,* conclude after extensive surveys and research that new alternatives to orthodoxy are emerging among America's religious people. They describe one aspect of the change as follows:

> The ethics of the new theologies differ sharply from the old. No longer are Christian ethics defined as matters of personal holiness or the rejection of private vices, but they are directed towards social justice, with the creation of a humane society.[20]

Thurman's concentration on the plight of the oppressed and disinherited, his concern for a social order governed by the love-ethic, and his vision of the inclusive community, indicate his sensitivity to this emerging concern. His piety does not condone the present political and social realities, but it feels a religious imperative to transform these realities.

Thurman's prophetic mysticism is of consequence to black religion in two ways. One, it is a vital alternative to the orthodoxy of most black religionists. The black religious tradition was deeply influenced by American evangelicalism. This evangelicalism stressed the divinity of Jesus, the ultimate authority of scriptures, and the supremacy of Christianity.[21] Even in the recent development of Black Theology these primary principles remain as the foundation of faith.

Thurman's modernistic liberalism and mysticism provide another distinct religious orientation from which to interpret the black religious experience. Though most black religion is grounded in American evangelicalism, Thurman's witness stands as a "minority report" to that tradition. His perspective not only provides diversity to the black religious tradition, in that he represents other blacks who share his theological tenets, but it also serves as a new reference for spiritual development within the black religious experience. His articulation of a liberal view offers blacks another theological option around which to rally their religious energies.

His liberal theology addresses the pressing problems which confront blacks, and it provides the intellectual framework for a proper sense of self and urge toward community. It reinterprets the relationship of Jesus to the oppressed, and it finds within the Negro spirituals sources of religious faith and hope. Mystical experience can give blacks a sense of their worth, mission, source of ultimate meaning and power, personal identity, and relationship to God.[22] Thurman's witness offers new credibility to religious liberalism and mysticism as systems of thought which are useful in the development of a theology which speaks to the

206

conditions of blacks in America.

The second consequence of Thurman's thought is its precursory relationship to Liberation and Black Theology. Liberation Theology focuses on the love and power of God which are functioning among the oppressed for their salvation—salvation from dehumanizing life conditions, and salvation to respond fully to God's purposes for humanity. Black Theology is a specific branch of Liberation Theology which appropriates the liberation themes to black Americans. These two recent theologies claim to: 1) reinterpret God's relationship to the poor and to proclaim God's activity in their liberation, 2) radically interpret Jesus as one of the oppressed whose ministry was to the oppressed, 3) offer a new Christian witness, siding with the struggles of the poor and oppressed, and 4) see the poor and oppressed as sources of revelation of what God is doing in the world.

After studying Thurman's theological development with these concepts, it becomes clear that his thought is a precursor to these theologies. This is a contribution which has been ignored by scholars who trace Liberation Theology to the work of Jurgen Moltmann, and Black Theology to James Cone. Years ahead of these two theologians, Thurman had already proclaimed and developed a religious philosophy based upon the above four tenets.

Direct evidence of Moltmann's familiarity with Thurman's thought cannot be found.

Within the works of Cone, however, are several references to Thurman's *Jesus and the Disinherited, Deep River,* and *The Negro Spiritual Speaks of Life and Death.*[23] Cone calls Thurman's interpretation of Jesus a "definition" which is "consistent with the black struggle for liberation."[24] He also credits Thurman as "one of the first scholars to use religion as the starting point in his [Thurman's] analysis of the black spirituals."[25] Cone occasionally utilizes Thurman's analysis to support his own scholarship with Negro spirituals.

Common interest in the significance of Jesus to the disinherited, concern for the liberation of the oppressed, and an appreciation of the spirituals as religious resources are the extent of any theological connection between Cone and Thurman. Thurman is a mystic theologian whose primary commitment is to reconciliation. Cone is an orthodox theologian whose commitment is to black liberation.

Thurman's prophetic mysticism stresses the formation of community through a liberation process that includes inner freedom. Inward liberation is not only a prerequisite for social transformation, it preserves the revolutionary sense of purpose after social transformation. Inward liberation keeps struggle (means) from being confused as the objective (ends).

The fight for voting rights was not just to give black people the opportunity to vote, but for them to exercise that right in reshaping the society. The fight for integrated schools was not just to have open admission policies, but for blacks to pursue quality education. After social and education barriers are reduced to a level where one can realistically compete and function in society, the motivation for struggle, meaning, and fulfillment should not be lost. In concentrating on "the hunger of the spirit," Thurman identifies this as the basis for keeping the vital sense of purpose, ends, and ultimate values.

This view is shared by Lerone Bennett, Jr., Senior Editor of *Ebony* magazine. In an editorial entitled "The Crisis of the Black Spirit," Bennett assesses the present situation of black youth and bemoans: the homicide which blacks have committed against one another, their improper sense of self, the absence of respect for others, the loss of direction and hope, the refusal to struggle for achievement, and the absence of a disciplined life which leads to excellence. Bennett articulates the severity of the "crisis" as follows:

> The danger is real and pressing. For the first time in our history, the inner fortresses of the Black Spirit are giving away. For the first time in history, we are threatened on the level of the spirit, on the level of our most precious possession, on the level of the soul.
>
> And what this means is that we are threatened today in this country as

we have never been threatened before. A Great Black Depression and policies of malign neglect are eroding the material foundations of our communities, and the fallout from this is eroding the moral and spiritual foundations of Black culture.

To come right out with it, *we are losing a whole generation of people.* And this fact, which is cultural, political and economic at the same time, constitutes the gravest challenge we have faced in this country since the end of slavery.[26]

The "spiritual crisis" theme is fleshed out in Rev. Jesse Jackson's PUSH for Excellence campaign. The campaign identifies public education as the breeding ground for the values which shape society. The basic assumptions of the campaign resemble Thurman's spiritual interpretation for the health of the social order:

Since academic performance continues to decline both for inner city and suburban youngsters, he [Jackson] believes a renewal of spirit, a revival of hope in the future, a resurrection of faith, a new resolve and determination to overcome, a restoration of the will to learn are desperately needed in the nation's schools.[27]

The Thurman-Bennett-Jackson principle is that inner development ultimately determines the destiny of a people. Racism and economic exploitation are crucial forces

210

which must be attacked, but too often they are perceived as forces external to the oppressed individual. The problems are always construed as "out there" in the system, outside the sufferer's responsibility. Consequently, one begins to accept one's condition as completely determined by the external forces. As Thurman says, the loss of responsibility leads to the loss of initiative over one's life, and the loss of initiative is the loss of human freedom, and the loss of human freedom results in slavery.

Thurman's interpretation of the spiritual basis for social transformation may serve as the philosophy for the next generation of participants in the black struggle. His prophetic spirituality addresses the inertia which befalls a revolution that has victories over legal and systemic injustices. With the destruction of easily identifiable targets of injustice, the question emerges: "Where do we go from here?" Thurman provides the goal when he speaks about self-actualization (reconciliation within the individual) and the urge toward community (reconciliation within society). Thurman understands liberation's purpose to be reconciliation; it is to take one beyond the reaction identity to realizing one's purpose within the ultimate movement of the universe.

Historically, social activism has been informed by the philosophy of persons who were not themselves activists. Henry David Thoreau is a prime example. He too was not an organization man, yet his ideas about social change influenced Mahatma Gandhi's India independence movement and Martin Luther King's leadership in civil rights. In a similar way, Thurman's theological treatments of nonviolence, spirituality in the social order, the religious resources within the oppressed, and the inclusive community may serve as the philosophical *elan vital* for future generations of social reformers.

Thurman's greatest legacy may be his vision of inclusive community. His vision of community is based on reconciliation which recognizes and celebrates the underlying unity of life and the inter-dependence of all life forms. Justice and a sense of innate equality are ruling principles for this community. And the love-ethic establishes and maintains the community's creative character. Personal identity is affirmed while unity is sought with one's fellows.

Thurman's inclusive community harbors all races, classes, faith claims, and ethnic groups; for in the eyes of God, every human is God's beloved child. Differences among people are not ignored or deprecated, though their importance does not overshadow the bond of kinship between individuals. Because of this bond, differences can be appreciated, rather than feared, for the variety of truth perspectives they bring to understanding. In cultural pluralism persons come to know the many faces of God, and what God is doing through diverse ways. Hopefully, this will give individuals a proper sense of self and neighbor such that one does not fall into destructive righteousness. Inclusive community confirms what Thurman understands as God's will for human relationships.

Thurman's vision is not only for the social order of the state, but for religious community. It is here that he labored to provide models which tested the validity of his beliefs. He proved that barriers to inclusive community could be overcome. These experiences of religious community stand as a significant challenge to the "will to segregate" which still dominates most church life. As it has been said: "Sunday morning is the most segregated hour in American life."[26]

Thurman's witness communicates an ideal which stretches all boundaries of community. The witness offers a goal for and beyond the immediate liberation struggle. The witness proclaims a mission for the social order and religious community which is commensurate with human potential. To paraphrase Thurman, the witness "places a crown above our heads which we can strive to grow tall enough to wear."

Thurman's convictions about the possibility for actualizing this inclusive community suggest two concepts integral to his thought: optimism and hope. His optimism hinges on the belief that God is in creation working toward harmony, completion, and the highest good. This innate force makes good more compelling than evil, relatedness more compelling than self-centeredness, and the

213

ultimate realization of community more probable than continued conflict and isolation. Thurman points to increasing knowledge, the evolutionary process, and the myths which inspire cultures as evidence that integral to life is the urge for the better, for wholeness.[29]

This optimism, which is basic to his theology and vision of community, is one of Thurman's most vulnerable tenets. Increasing knowledge has not only brought healing and understanding, but a technology which can annihilate life. While nature holds designs of growth and harmony, there are inexplicable disorders which cause nature to turn on itself. While cultures treasure dreams of cooperation and well-being, history is replete with cultures whose inspiration was control, domination, and exploitation. Even where the human will is properly motivated, insanity remains a constant threat. All these difficulties do not cancel the beloved community, but they do challenge Thurman's optimism as a sound basis for its realization.

More profound is Thurman's sense of hope. His hope is derived from the feeling of security, power, and meaning received through religious experience. Thurman's mysticism, his reliance upon the God-encounter, assured him that love can be experienced in the midst of hate, meaning in chaos, peace in the midst of turmoil, fulfillment in non-supportive circumstances, and unity and wholeness within separateness and fragmentation. God can provide the sense of community even though conditions and forces would seek to prevent it.[30]

This *confidence* in the ultimate power of God does not exclude a progressive movement toward the world's transformation into the beloved community, but neither does it guarantee it. God is the ground of community, and this knowledge should sustain commitments and labors on its behalf. Through hope one realizes that God brings purpose and salvation. Though humanity may destroy itself, life is still ultimately in God's caring hands. In this assurance our spirits can take comfort. Thurman has this sense of hope, and it is somewhat ironic that he also maintains the optimism.

The future remembers. The destiny of community is related to past realities. The reality of Howard Thurman must be kept available to future generations, not for the purpose of honoring Thurman, but for the nourishing and renewing of the people. Ignored prophets may be more a judgment on the wisdom of their communities than the validity of the prophetic message. Communities are stewards of creative precepts and examples which stimulate growth, prevent stagnation, and cultivate the resources of God's creation. They are stewards who hold the difference between promised land and wasteland realities. The faithful execution of this responsibility determines the prophetic community.

In his *The Search for Common Ground,*

Thurman anticipates new opportunities to experience inclusive community when he writes:

> It is time for assessing and reassessing resources in the light of the most ancient memory of the race concerning community, to hear again the clear voice of prophet and seer calling for harmony among all the children of men. At length there will begin to be talk of plans for the new city—that has never before existed on land or sea.[31]

He continues the vision by saying:

> One day there will stand up in their midst one who will tell of a new sickness among the children who in their delirium cry for their brothers whom they have never known and from whom they have been cut off behind the self-imposed barriers of their fathers. An alarm will spread throughout the community that it is being felt and slowly realized that community cannot feed for long on itself; it can only flourish where always the boundaries are giving way to the coming of others from beyond them—unknown and undiscovered brothers.[32]

Though he was not speaking of himself, his witness has functioned in this way. Though other prophetic voices come and transform the land into community, they will be indebted to a prophetic lineage—a lineage which includes Howard Thurman.

One of Thurman's favorite quotations is Petrarch's: "if those whom it behooves to speak are silent, let any speak that the truth may be served." When the boundaries of community were confined and restricted until they suffocated life, Howard Thurman was not silent. He continues to be heard and to make a difference.

NOTES

Chapter I

1. Lerone Bennett, Jr. , "Howard Thurman: 20th Century Holy Man," *Ebony*, February 1978, p. 68.

2. Two studies on Thurman which demonstrate extensive research and good scholarship are Irving Moxley's "An Examination of the Mysticism of Howard Thurman and Its Relevance to Black Liberation," D. Min. Paper, Louisville Presbyterian Theological Seminary, June 1974; and Mozella G. Mitchell's "The Dynamics of Howard Thurman's Relationship to Literature and Theology," Ph.D. Dissertation, Emory University, August 1980. [Since the 1981 publication of this book, there have been three scholarly books that have focused on Thurman's thought and contributions: Mozella G. Mitchell's *Spiritual Dynamics of Howard Thurman's Theology* (Wyndham Hall Press, 1985); Walter E. Fluker's *They Looked for a City: A Comparative Analysis of the Ideal of Community in the Thought of Howard Thurman and Martin Luther King, Jr.* (University Press of America, 1989); and Carlyle Fielding Stewart, III's, *God, Being and Liberation: A Comparative Analysis of the Theologies and Ethics of James H. Cone and Howard Thurman* (University Press of America, 1989).]

3. Herbert Warren Richardson, "Martin Luther King-Unsung Theologian," in *New Theology* No. 6, eds. Martin E. Marty and Dean G. Peerman (London: Collier-Macmillan, 1969), p. 184.

4. Luther E. Smith, Jr. interview with Howard Thurman, Howard Thurman Educational Trust Office, San Francisco, California, 13 June 1977.

5. Howard Thurman, *Footprints of a Dream: The Story of the Church for the Fellowship of All Peoples* (New York: Harper & Brothers, 1959), p. 21.

6. *Ibid.*, p. 22.

218

7. Smith interview with Thurman, 13 June 1977.

8. *Ibid.*

9. While Thurman was a youth, Mordecai Johnson inspired him with one of his addresses. Thurman then wrote Johnson for advice on planning his education. Johnson's impact and counsel were important influences with Thurman during his formative years. One might speculate that this personal respect and endearment also entered into Thurman's decision to accept the Howard position. See Elizabeth Yates, *Howard Thurman: Portrait of a Practical Dreamer* (New York: John Day, 1964), pp. 47-48.

10. Yates, *Howard Thurman*, p. 95.

11. Thurman, *Footprints of a Dream*, p. 24.

12. *Ibid.*, p. 24.

13. When Thurman was first contacted about the church, he was being asked to recommend persons who might serve in a co-pastorate. In responding to this initial inquiry he commended the efforts of the church for attempting such a pioneering effort. The church's pastor was so taken with Thurman's support that he immediately corresponded with Thurman asking him to consider accepting the position. Insights into the change which led to Thurman's move to San Francisco can be found in, *The First Footprints: The Dawn of the Idea of The Church for the Fellowship of All Peoples: Letters Between Alfred Fisk & Howard Thurman, 1943-1944* (San Francisco: Lawton and Alfred Kennedy, 1975).

14. Thurman, *The First Footprints*, p. 46.

15. Even after Fisk's other responsibilities required his resignation, the church intentionally hired white clergy in order to maintain inter-racial leadership. Thurman carried primary responsibility for the church's ministerial leadership. See *Footprints of a Dream*, pp. 98, 100, 102-103.

16. Thurman, *Footprints of a Dream*, p. 109.

17. *Ibid.*, p. 125.

18. While Thurman was pleased with the impact and accomplishments of Fellowship Church, he recognized, in retrospect, that some different approaches might have provided more stability for the church.

One change related to the nurturing of young adults for the church. Since he was primarily known in California (before coming to Fellowship Church) among college youth, he was apprehensive about the church becoming crowded with these students. He felt that a dominance of "Thurman's group" might diminish the significant statement the church could make to the larger society; it would always be labeled as having an artificial character. So he discouraged any efforts to increase the church's membership by drawing upon his appeal to college students. He reflected that this decision may have harmed the ongoing life of Fellowship Church. The church did not have this category of membership which would add children, attract other youth, and give the church a longer living (more stable) membership.

Thurman also felt that after Fellowship Church proved its convictions about an inter-racial fellowship, it might have acquired more stability by joining one of the "historic denominations." This would have given the church "anchorage" while it maintained its "freedom." The joining of a denomination could have provided a variety of support services to meet the kinds of difficulties which every church must confront. Fellowship Church has continued to this day, but at times its ongoing viability has been very precarious. See Luther E. Smith, Jr. interview with Howard Thurman, Indianapolis, Indiana, November 1975.

19. Howard Thurman, "Mysticism and Social Action," the Lawrence Lecture on Religion and Society (First Unitarian Church of Berkeley), 13 October 1978.

20. Howard Thurman, "Mysticism and Social Change," *Eden Theological Seminary Bulletin* IV (Spring Quarter, 1939):27.

21. Segundo Galilea, "Liberation as an Encounter with Politics and Contemplation," in *The Mystical and Political Dimension of the Christian Faith,* eds. Claude Geffre and Gustavo Gutierrez (New York: Herder and Herder, 1974), p. 28.

22. *Ibid.*, pp. 31-32.

Chapter II

1. The investigation does not attempt to discuss every important influence in Thurman's life; this would include a long list of teachers (elementary, high school, and college), friends, books, and experiences. The four persons examined in this chapter provide major insights which continuously influenced his thought. The reader may question the omission of Olive Schreiner as a pivotal figure; particularly since Thurman edited and published her writings. Schreiner's stories are a creative source of inspiration to him; her emphasis on the unity of all life is a major theme in Thurman's thought. This writer's analysis, however, is that she *expresses* what Thurman already feels and believes, rather than contributing new theological perspectives to the foundation of his thought. This is not to deny that she nourishes his thinking. Certainly, her articulation of the "unity" theme has a major influence upon Thurman. It does, however, place her significance in another category.

2. Jean Burden, "Howard Thurman," *Atlantic*, October 1953, p. 39.

3. Smith interview with Thurman 13 June 1977.

4. George Cross, *What Is Christianity: A Study of Rival Interpretations* (Chicago: University of Chicago Press, 1918), p. vii.

5. *Ibid.* , p. 173.

6. *Ibid.* , p. 187. A thorough study of theologies, throughout the Church's history, which have attempted to define Christianity's "essence" is found in William Adams Brown's *The Essence of Christianity: A Study in the History of Definition* (New York: Charles Scribner's Sons, 1913).

7. The term "higher life" is loosely defined by Cross; the context of his use for this term implies "a better life," "an improved life," "a more honest and truthful Life," "a more complete and satisfying life."

8. Cross, *What is Christianity*, p.193. Ernst Troeltsch, a late nineteenth century theologian, is

critical of this understanding concerning the "essence" of Christianity. Troeltsch provides an excellent critique in his *The Absoluteness of Christianity and the History of Religions*, trans. David Reid, with an Introduction by James Luther Adams (Richmond,VA.: John Knox Press, 1971), pp. 62-83.

9. Cross, *What is Christianity*, pp. 172-204.

10. George Cross, *Christian Salvation: A Modern Interpretation* (Chicago: University of Chicago Press, 1925), p. 133.

11. George Cross, *Creative Christianity: A Study of the Genius of the Christian Faith* (New York: MacMillan Co., 1922), pp. 8 and 49.

12. *Ibid.*, p. 55. In this book, *Christian Salvation*, Cross says that "personality" is such a complex term, it is indefinable. He offers, however, a definition which may yield some sense of the meaning of the term: "It is the ultimate in our search for the source of all feeling, knowledge or action. Personality is that which is self-conscious in all the forms of our consciousness. Personality, self-consciousness is and apart from it we cannot say that any thing else exists." (p. 144).

13. Evangelical liberalism is part of the religious liberalism tradition. William Ernest Hocking provides a precise definition of religious liberalism, which helps in understanding the context of evangelical liberalism. In his essay, "The Meaning of Liberalism: An Essay in Definition," in *Liberal Theology: An Appraisal*, eds. David E. Roberts and Henry Pitney Van Dusen (New York: Charles Scribner's Sons, 1942), Hocking says, "But liberalism is not to be identified with any particular dissent, nor with dissent as such, but only with dissent from the view that any version of Christianity is *all final*. Finality there is and must be finality in religion, or else religion fails of its primary task: to give man a point of stability. But to say that any version is all final is to deny that there is room for growth in apprehension, which is itself an unchristian view. Christianity, in its doctrine of the Holy Spirit, is pre-eminently the religion of growth; and liberalism in this sense is the only

possible orthodoxy." (p. 57) Chapter III will focus on the types of religious liberalism. Hocking offers a broad definition which will help characterize Howard Thurman's religious tradition.

14. Kenneth Cauthen, *The Impact of American Religious Liberalism* (New York: Harper & Row, 1962), pp. 27-28.

15. The emphasis which Cross places on this "personality-centered Christianity" is strongly stated in his book *Creative Christianity*, pp. 52-53.

16. Landrum Bolling interview with Howard Thurman, Howard Thurman Educational Trust Office, San Francisco, California, 8 and 9 January 1976.

17. Smith interview with Thurman, 13 June 1977.

18. Yates, *Howard Thurman*, pp. 78-79.

19. Howard Thurman does not remember ever going to Robins's office; he did not have the kind of close relationship with Robins, as he had with Cross. Along with the chapel meditations, Thurman was impressed by Robins's articles in the *Rochester Bulletin*.

20. Smith interview with Thurman, 13 June 1977.

21. Burden, "Howard Thurman," p. 40.

22. Cross was also very interested in the status of Christianity as it relates to other religions. This comparison highlights the emphases of these two authors; or more pertinent to this discussion, the emphasis of their impact on Howard Thurman.

23. Troeltsch, in *The Absoluteness of Christianity*, characterizes this relationship when he says: "This 'essence of Christianity,' moreover, is thought of as related to the concrete individual forms of the Christian religion in the same way that the essence of religion is related to the concrete religions. Just as these religions must be understood on the basis of the universal principle that is imminent within them, so Christianity must be understood on the basis of the universal principle that is realized in it" (p. 66). Troeltsch immediately initiates a sharp criticism of this view. This criticism reflects Thurman's departure from Cross and Robins—a departure which will be discussed in Chapter III.

24. Robins believes that Christianity has the "Supreme Pattern" of the moral personality in "The Lord Jesus Christ." In his *Four Addresses before the Burma Baptist Mission Conference* (Rangoon: American Baptist Mission Press, 1928), Robins assures the Conference that they represent a faith which can demonstrate its ability to meet the needs of humanity in any cultural context. He does not present this with any hard line evangelism, which negates any value in the present religious status of those who do not profess Christianity. Robins is not interested in stressing the need to have the world confess Jesus Christ as Lord and Savior, but in having Christians to demonstrate the superior life-style which comes with Christianity—that Christianity is the most accessible road to the "higher life." Robins is also aware that Christianity is not predestined to retain its superior status in the world. If the "essence" of the faith is to survive, there must be considerable labor to keep Christianity vital to cultural needs. Among one of Robins's fuller writings is his *Concerning Culture and the Future of Religion,* reprinted from The *Colgate-Rochester Divinity School Bulletin,* November 1931, in which he outlines how various religions have been molders of and molded by culture. Culture makes common demands upon any religion; the success (lasting power) of religion depends upon its ability to satisfy these demands. Christianity is not exempt from this requirement. It can fail and enter the category of "dead religions." This failure would not be a reflection upon its essence, but upon the bearers of the essence (p. 8).

25. Robins's definition of the "saved community" follows the same general pattern as Cross's definition. They stress an environment for the growth of personality. A "friendly universe, a world in which one can hope and move forward unafraid," is a phrase used in his article, "The Unseen World," *The Rochester Theological Seminary Bulletin,* reprinted from The 76th Annual Report, 76:3, p. 11. This friendly world is based on moral principles which stress love and justice.

26. Robins, "Unseen World," pp. 8, 10, and 12.

27. Smith interview with Thurman, 13 June 1977.

28. *Ibid.*

29. Rufus M. Jones, *Studies in Mystical Religion* (London: MacMillan and Co., 1923), p. xv.

30. Rufus M. Jones, *Rufus Jones Speaks to Our Time*, ed. Harry Emerson Fosdick (New York: MacMillan Co., 1951), p. 204.

31. *Ibid.*, p. 160.

32. *Rufus Jones Speaks to Our Time* is an excellent source for receiving Jones's theology, particularly as it covers a wide range of subjects. Another good source is Jones's *Social Law in the Spiritual World: Studies in Human and Divine Inter-Relationship* (Philadelphia: John C. Winston Co., 1904).

33. Cross, in *What Is Christianity*, expresses an appreciation for mysticism. His major criticism of this tradition is its resistance to being involved in social and political issues (p. 85). It is, therefore, ironic that among these three men, Jones is the strongest advocate of mysticism, and the most outspoken on social and political involvement.

34. Howard Thurman, *Mysticism and the Experience of Love* (Wallingford, PA.: Pendle Hill, 1961), pp. 4-5.

35. *Ibid.*, p. 3.

36. Jones also uses the term "Kingdom of God" to express the state of a saved world. See H. Richard Niebuhr's *The Kingdom of God in America* (New York: Harper & Row, 1937). Niebuhr's classic traces the ideal of creating God's Kingdom on earth, specifically on American soil for the salvation of the world. Cross, Robins, and Jones do not appear to have the nationalism critiqued by Niebuhr; but they do not lack any of the vision that the coming of the Kingdom is a matter of human volition and effort. This "willing in" the Kingdom of God is a major feature of the Social Gospel movement which takes place during the last half of the nineteenth Century. The prevailing feeling is that humanity can not only take initiative for developing its salvation, but it can achieve its salvation. This differs from humanism in

that the source of one's power and authority is understood to be God. It puts no less responsibility on humanity, however, to create an eschatological time and place.

37. Jones, *Rufus Jones*, p. 10.

38. Cauthen, *Religious Liberalism*, p. 36.

39. Yates, *Howard Thurman*, p. 84.

40. In the 13 June 1977 Smith interview with Dr. Thurman, he stated that even though his mother remarried twice, there was always an agreement between her and his grandmother that the men would not have any responsibility for rearing him; he was to be the sole responsibility of his mother and grandmother.

41. Mary E. Goodwin, "Racial Roots and Religion: An Interview with Howard Thurman," *Christian Century*, 9 May 1973, p. 533.

42. Yates, *Howard Thurman*, pp. 30-48.

43. Roberta Byrd Barr, interview with Howard Thurman, Seattle, Washington, January 1969.

44. Howard Thurman, "Standing Inside with Christ," a lecture given at Bishop College: Lacey Kirk Institute, April 21, 1970.

45. Goodwin, "Racial Roots," p. 533.

46 Jones's contribution in dealing with the social order is the next step up; one can focus on transforming conditions, if he or she can survive their destructive effects.

47. Goodwin, "Racial Roots," p. 533.

48. *Ibid.*, p. 534.

49. Nancy Ambrose's influence can be seen in Thurman's book, *Jesus and the Disinherited* (Nashville: Abingdon-Cokesbury Press, 1949). Thurman gives an interpretation of Jesus which asks and answers the question: "What does the religion of Jesus have to say to those who have their backs against the wall?"

50. In an article entitled "Jesus Christ in Howard Thurman's Thought," John D. Mangram considers the absence of Thurman material on the Apostle Paul, as "one of the most glaring weaknesses of Thurman's view of Jesus." (See *Common Ground*, Gandy (ed.), p. 75.) Mangram's observation on Thurman not

226

focusing on the contributions of Paul toward an understanding of Jesus is correct. But this is not an oversight on Thurman's part, it is deliberate. In Thurman's mind, Paul was a privileged Jew (being a Roman citizen) who was not as sensitive as Jesus to the disinherited's plight. Secondly, Paul's dogma does not appeal to Thurman. It indicates the attempts of a man who was trying to make sense from his religious experience through symbols and doctrine. Thurman sees it as an effort to compensate for the lack of primary contact with Jesus, and to justify his right as an Apostle. The influence of Nancy Ambrose is all the more evident when one realizes that she forbade Thurman to read to her from the writings of Paul, except for I Corinthians 13. I Corinthians 13 is the only Pauline passage given considerable treatment by Thurman in his writings and speaking.

51. The 139th Psalm was one of Nancy Ambrose's favorite passages of scripture; it became Thurman's favorite. The Psalm is often considered to represent a mystic's view of the God-human relationship. For a treatment on this Psalm, as it relates to mystical experience, see Dorothee Soelle's *Death By Bread Alone: Texts and Reflections on Religious Experience,* trans. David L. Scheidt (Philadelphia: Fortress Press, 1978), pp. 119-126.

52. Howard Thurman, *The Luminous Darkness* (New York: Harper & Row, 1965), p. 3. See also Yates, *Howard Thurman,* p. 68.

Chapter III

1. Samuel Lucius Gandy, ed., *Common Ground: Essays in Honor of Howard Thurman* on the Occasion of His Seventy-fifth Birthday, November 18, 1975, with Forewords by Kenneth I. Brown, Benjamin E. Mays, and Douglas V. Steere (Washington, D.C.: Hoffman Press, 1976).

2. Ralph G. Turnbull, *A History of Preaching,* volume 3 (Grand Rapids, MI: Baker Book House, 1974), p. 206.

3. Joseph R. Washington, Jr., *Black Religion: The Negro and Christianity in the United States* (Boston: Beacon Press, 1964), pp. 105 and 111.

4. Gandy, ed., *Common Ground*, p. 65.

5. Allen O. Miller, *Invitation to Theology: Resources for Christian Nurture and Discipline* (Philadelphia: Christian Education Press, 1958), pp. 4, 5, and 7-8.

6. Barr interview with Thurman.

7. This writer has not detected any major shifts in Thurman's writing over the last forty-five years. His book *Disciplines of the Spirit* (1963) is the first full treatment given the theme of the inter-related universe; his *The Search for Common Ground* (1971) is a further development of this theme which continually emerges and gathers evidence for the claims of community.

8. Howard Thurman, *The Search for Common Ground: An Inquiry into the Basis of Man's Experience of Community* (New York: Harper & Row, 1971), pp. xi, xii, 76, and 77.

9. *Disciplines of the Spirit*, pp. 104-105. Thurman, in his *A Track to the Water's Edge: The Olive Schreiner Reader* (New York: Harper & Row, 1973), pp. xxvii-xxviii, credits Olive Schreiner as a writer who had a major influence in nurturing this concept for his mind.

10. Rudolf Otto, *Mysticism East and West: A Comparative Analysis of the Nature of Mysticism*, trans. Berthan L. Bracey and Richenda C. Payne (New York: Macmillan Co., 1932), pp. 44-45.

11. Thurman, *The Search for Common Ground*, p. 6.

12. Thurman often uses the term "Life" to represent the vitality of the universe. This vitality is in all creation; it gives meaning to existence and assures new possibilities.

13. Thurman, *Disciplines*, p, 122.

14. Howard Thurman, *Deep Is the Hunger: Meditations for Apostles of Sensitiveness* (New York: Harper & Brothers, 1951), p. 109.

15. Thurman, *The Search for Common Ground*, pp. 83-84.

16. This theme is very evident throughout the writings of Cross and Jones. One also finds it to be a major concept of New England transcendentalism. Transcendentalism is the closest American movement to European romanticism. An excellent connection between transcendentalism and liberal theology is made in Frederick Sontag and John K. Roth's *The American Religious Experience: The Roots, Trends, and Future of American Theology* (New York: Harper & Row, 1972), pp. 65-95.

17. Otto makes distinctions between the terms "Unity" and "Oneness" in mystical theology. These terms can be related in three ways: 1) Unity means inter-relationship, such that the "(mystical) synthesis of multiplicity" reveals the Oneness of the universe; Unity discloses and affirms Oneness. 2) There develops from this first definition the sense that "out of the united comes the One only, out of the All-One the Alone"; Unity is lost to Oneness. And 3) Unity is no longer immanent in the One, for the One transcends Unity, and Unity becomes "wholly evil in contrast to the realm of the One"; Unity negates Oneness. (Otto, *Mysticism*, pp. 51-52) Thurman's concern for community emphasizes the first definition where Unity and Oneness are inter-changeable.

18. Howard Thurman, *The Inward Journey* (New York: Harper & Row, 1961), pp. 34-35.

19. Howard Thurman, "What Can We Believe In?" reprinted from *Journal of Religion and Health* (April 1973): 114.

20. Kenneth Cauthen speaks to this tenet in his *The Impact of American Religious Liberalism* when he describes the theology of Harry Emerson Fosdick, another noted evangelical liberal: "He [Fosdick] begins with man—his experiences, his values, and his worth—not with God—his will, his revelation, and his actions. God is understood in terms of man, not man in terms of God. This anthropocentric tendency is widespread in liberalism." (p. 74).

21. Friedrich Schleiermacher, *On Religion: Speeches to its Cultured Despisers*, trans. John Oman with an

Introduction by Rudolf Otto (New York: Harper & Row, 1958), pp. 36 and 41.

22. Thurman, *Deep Is the Hunger*, p. 62.

23. *Ibid.*, p. 63.

24. *Ibid.*, p. 109.

25. Thurman, *Inward Journey*, p. 40.

26. Thurman, "What Can We Believe In?" p. 117.

27. Thurman, *Deep Is the Hunger*, pp. 94-95.

28. Thurman, "What Can We Believe In?" p. 117.

29. Lloyd J. Averill, *American Theology in the Liberal Tradition* (Philadelphia: Westminster Press, 1967), p. 74.

30. Paul Tillich, *A History of Christian Thought: From Its Judaic and Hellenistic Origins to Existentialism*, ed. Carl E. Braaten (New York: Simon and Schuster, 1967), p. 377.

31. Thurman, *Inward Journey*, pp. 34-35.

32. Howard Thurman, "The Sources of Tradition-Part III," a sermon delivered at Marsh Chapel on 11 October 1959.

33. Thurman, "What Can We Believe In?" p. 114. Another statement on the nature of evil, which is tied to a biblical account of this problem, is in Thurman's "Exposition to The Book of Habakkuk" in *The Interpreter's Bible*, Vol. VI, eds. George Arthur Buttrick et al. (New York: Abingdon Press, 1956), p. 986.

34. Thurman's concepts on evil are representative of mystical theology; see Alan Watts *Behold the Spirit: A Study in the Necessity of Mystical Religion* (New York: Vintage Books, 1972), pp. 148-152.

35. Howard Thurman, "Varieties of Peace," meditation tape.

36. An example of the refusal to consider the historical Jesus as a significant concern is found in Ralph Waldo Emerson's famous 1838 Divinity School Address; the Address can be found in *The American Tradition in Literature*, Fourth Edition, eds. Sculley Bradley, Richmond Croom Beatty, E. Hudon Long, and George Perkins, Vol. I (n.p.: Grosset & Dunlap, 1974), p. 1097.

37. Thurman, *Disinherited*, pp. 11-35.

38. This insight is particularly expressed in Thurman's meditation on Jesus' refusal to jump from the temple; see *Inward Journey*, pp. 55-56.

39. Thurman, *Deep Is the Hunger*, pp. 172-173.

40. Thurman, *Disinherited*, p. 15. Kenneth Cauthen indicates how much this is part of the tradition of liberalism when he says: "Liberalism was infused with a fresh enthusiasm for the historical origins of Christianity. It is in the moral teachings and the religious experience of Jesus himself that the essence of Christianity is to be found. Liberals began to make a distinction between the religion *of* Jesus and the religion *about* Jesus." (*Impact of American Religious Liberalism*, p. 65).

41. Howard Thurman, *The Growing Edge* (New York: Harper & Brothers, 1956), pp. 97-98.

42. Thurman, *Disinherited*, p. 21.

43. *Ibid.*, p. 49.

44. *Ibid.*, p. 102.

45. *Ibid.*, pp. 89-109.

46. Howard Thurman, "Mysticism and Jesus," lecture V given at the University of the Redlands, May 1973.

47. Howard Thurman, *The Mood of Christmas* (New York: Harper & Row, 1973), p. 10.

48. *Ibid.*, p. 9.

49. Thurman, *Disinherited*, p. 29.

50. Thurman, *Deep Is the Hunger*, pp. 171-172.

51. Thurman, *Growing Edge*, pp. 98-99. Jesus was the example, for the romanticists, of full God consciousness. Jesus' nature was no different than other human beings, but what he accomplished gave him persuasion over lives.

52. Howard Thurman *The Creative Encounter: An Interpretation of Religion and the Social Witness* (New York: Harper & Brothers, 1954), pp. 82-83.

53. Howard Thurman, "Mysticism and Social Change," pp. 12-13. During an interview with this writer (28 June 1976 at the Howard Thurman Educational Trust Office, San Francisco, California), Dr. Thurman indicated that he rarely closed his prayers

with "in the name of Jesus Christ our Lord"; and when he has said it, it has primarily been to meet the worship expectations of some of his audience.

54. Thurman, *Mood of Christmas*, p. 11.

55. Thurman, *Deep Is the Hunger*, p. 163.

56. *Ibid.*, p. 31.

57. Thurman, *Growing Edge*, pp. 130-137.

58. Thurman, *Deep is the Hunger*, p. 177.

59. See Howard Thurman, *Deep River and The Negro Spiritual Speaks of Life and Death* (Richmond, IN.: Friends United Press, 1945 and 1947), pp. 69-78,

60. Thurman, *Deep is the Hunger*, pp. 161-162.

61. Smith interview with Thurman, 13 June 1977.

62. Thurman, "Standing Inside with Christ."

63. Thurman, *Deep Is the Hunger*, p. 146.

64. Thurman, *Creative Encounter,* p. 28.

65. Thurman, *Inward Journey*, p. 133.

66. Thurman, *Disciplines*, pp. 87 and 93. In *History of Christian Thought* Tillich explains how this was a basic principle of romanticism. Within this movement it was expressed as "the finite is not only finite, but in some dimension it is also infinite and has the divine as its center and ground." (p. 374)

67. Panentheism is a term used by Charles Hartshorne and William L. Reese in their book *Philosophers Speak of God* (Chicago: The University of Chicago Press, 1953). Panentheism brings together the concepts of theism and pantheism to create a theology which accepts polar opposites as correlatives. The Supreme is therefore eternal *and* temporal, infinite *and* finite, one *and* many, immanent *and* transcendent, absolute *and* relative (pp. 15-17).

68. Thurman, "Mysticism and Social Change," p. 8. For the relationship of "God as personality" to Christianity, see Alan Watts's *Behold The Spirit*, pp. 159-160.

69. Thurman, *Growing Edge*, p. 65.

70. Thurman, *Deep Is the Hunger*, p. 146.

71. *Ibid.*, p. 94.

72. Howard Thurman, *Meditations of the Heart* (New York: Harper & Row, 1953), pp. 37-39.

73. Thurman, *Inward Journey*, pp. 137-138.

74. Thurman, "Mysticism and Social Change," p. 8. This concept is also integral to the tradition of mysticism. Underscoring the significance of love to religious experience, Evelyn Underhill in her book *Mysticism: A Study in the Nature and Development of Man's Spiritual Consciousness* (Cleveland: World Publishing Co., 1955), says: "A harmony is thus set up between the mystic and Life in all its forms. Undistracted by appearance, he sees, feels, and knows it in one piercing act of loving comprehension. . . . The heart outstrips the clumsy senses, sees—perhaps for an instant, perhaps for long periods of bliss—an undistorted and more veritable world. All things are perceived in the light of charity, and hence under the aspect of beauty: for beauty is simply Reality seen with the eyes of love." (p. 258)

75. Thurman, *Growing Edge*, p. 67.

76. Thurman, *Creative Encounter,* p. 20. Thurman's writings which are directed at defining and describing religious experience are: *The Creative Encounter* (this is his fullest treatment on the subject) "Mysticism and Social Change" (these lectures represent Thurman's first effort to systematically articulate his beliefs on mysticism), and *Mysticism and the Experience of Love.*

77. Thurman, *Disciplines*, p. 23. This premise is basic to Schleiermacher's system; see Tillich's *History of Christian Thought*, p. 395.

78. Douglas Clyde Macintosh, *The Problem of Religious Knowledge* (New York: Harper & Brothers, 1940), pp. 9-11.

79. *Ibid.*, pp. 15-28,

80. *Ibid.*, p. 6.

81. Thurman, *Creative Encounter*, pp. 20-26.

82. Walter T. Stace, *The Teachings of the Mystics* (New York: New American Library, 1960), p. 26.

83. Stace, *The Teachings*, p. 15.

84. Thurman, *Creative Encounter*, p. 30.

85. *Ibid.*, p. 30.

86. *Ibid.*, p. 65.

87. *Ibid.*, pp. 40 and 75.

88. Thurman, "Mysticism and Social Change," p.

30.

89. Thurman, *Creative Encounter*, pp. 123-124.

90. Thurman, *Inward Journey*, pp. 54-58.

91. These disciplines are extensively treated in Thurman's *Disciplines of the Spirit.*

92. Thurman, *Creative Encounter*, p. 34.

93. *Ibid.*, pp. 37-38 and 59.

94. *Ibid.*, p. 12.

95. *Ibid.*, pp. 140-145. A classic book which traces the social causes of church fragmentation and schism is Richard Niebuhr's *The Social Sources of Denominationalism* (New York: World Publishing Co., 1957).

96. *Ibid.*, p. 146.

97. *Ibid.*, pp. 135-142.

98. Howard Thurman, "What We Teach," unpublished presentation to the Church School Institute of Fellowship Church, n.d.

99. Thurman, *Creative Encounter*, pp. 147-148.

100. *Ibid.*, p. 150

101. Thurman's use of the Bible as a resource conforms to his theological bases. He states that Mark is his favorite Gospel: 1) because it is reported to be the oldest, and therefore perhaps the most reliable, and 2) it does not contain narratives on the miraculous birth of Jesus; Mark's emphasis is on the life and ministry of Jesus. As mentioned earlier, the supernatural is not stressed by Thurman.

102. Howard Thurman, "What We Teach."

103. Thurman, *Creative Encounter,* pp. 130-135.

104. Howard Thurman, "Sources of Tradition—Part IV," part of a sermon series delivered at Marsh Chapel at Boston University, 18 October 1959.

105. Thurman, *Deep Is the Hunger*, p. 39.

106. This connection with romanticism is especially pronounced as one looks at its and Thurman's concept of history. Tillich, in *A History of Christian Thought*, portrays the romanticist sense of history as follows: "The idea of the presence of the infinite in the finite gave Romanticism the possibility of a new relationship to the past . . . . The infinite was also present in the past periods of history through expres-

sive forms of life and their great symbols. They had their revelatory character also. This means that history, the historical past, be taken seriously." (p. 380) Thurman, in *Deep Is the Hunger* says: "A fresh sense of history must be developed. All the events of the world must be placed in a context of incident that reveals their profound interrelatedness. . .History is not irrational; it has a deep logic and consistency. God is the God of history. He does not stand apart as some mighty spectator but is in the process and the facts ever shaping them. . ." (p. 2)

107. Cross, *What is Christianity*, pp. 193-194.

108. Jones, *Speaks to Our Time*, pp. 10, 47, and 191.

109. Henry B. Robins, *Aspects of Authority in Christian Religion* (Philadelphia: Griffith & Rowland Press, 1911), pp. 138-140, 145-146.

110. Henry B. Robins, "Christian Progress in the Far East: A Report of a Visit to Baptist Mission Fields in Japan, China and the Philippine Islands, 1920-1921" (New York: American Baptist Foreign Mission Society), p. 4.

111. Cauthen, *Impact of American Religious Liberalism,* p. 29.

112. Howard Thurman, *The Luminous Darkness: A Personal Interpretation of the Anatomy of Segregation and the Ground of Hope* (New York: Harper & Row, 1965), p. 112.

113. Cauthen, *Impact of American Religious Liberalism*, p. 30.

114. See Macintosh, *Religious Knowledge*, pp. 188-213.

115. Thurman, *Creative Encounter*, p. 147.

116. Joseph Glaser, Memorial Services tribute to Howard Thurman, San Francisco, California, 16 April 1981.

117. Paul Tillich, *Christianity and the Encounter of the World Religions* (New York: Columbia University Press, 1963), p. 97.

118. Thurman, *The Search for Common Ground*, pp. 78-84.

119. *Ibid.*, pp. 78-84.

120. Earl H. Brill, *The Creative Edge of American Protestantism* (New York: Seabury Press, 1966), p. 3.

121. See Irving H. Bartlett's, *The American Mind in the Mid-Nineteenth Century* (New York: Thomas Y. Crowdell Co., 1967), pp. 1-72.

122. *Ibid.*, p. 25.

123. Sydney E. Ahlstrom, *A Religious History of the American People* (New Haven: Yale University Press, 1972), p. 1019.

124. An extensive study of the various success and improvement themes found in harmonial religion is part of Louis Schneider and Sanford M. Dorbusch's *Popular Religion: Inspirational Books in America* (Chicago: The University of Chicago Press, 1958).

125. Thurman explains Jesus' oppression as a condition which befalls him, not because of any initiative upon his part, but because of the exploiting and dehumanizing character of the Roman Empire. (See *Jesus and the Disinherited*, pp. 18-23.)

126. The Social Gospel Movement is heralded as a theological development which seriously related the social condition of the country to the hope of establishing the Kingdom of God. The plight of the poor, immigrants, labor, and those alienated by urbanization became the concern of this movement's mission. The socio-economic problems of black Americans were not, however, given attention by this movement's proponents. Neither have other theologians (until the emergence of Black Theology in the late 1960s) taken the conditions of black Americans as a crucial context for understanding the work and faithfulness of Christianity.

Chapter IV

1. While Thurman consistently comments on black/white relations, this is not his only social concern. He has also spoken to the plight of Jews, Japanese-Americans, Native Americans, India's Untouchables, and other oppressed groups. The black struggle, however, has personally affected and in-

236

volved his life to a greater degree, providing the primary context for his social witness.

2. Howard Thurman, "Good News for the Underprivileged," *Religion in Life*, Summer Issue (1935), pp. 403-409.

3. Thurman, *Disinherited*, p. 7.

4. *Ibid.*, p. 34.

5. American theologians, representing the views of the culture, have portrayed Jesus as resembling their self-image. If they were conservative, Jesus was a conservative; if they were liberal, Jesus was a liberal; if they were success oriented, Jesus was success oriented (i.e., Bruce Barton's *The Man Nobody Knows* and Norman Vincent Peale's *The Power of Positive Thinking*); if they had concern for social transformation, Jesus had concern for social transformation. Surely their approach did not differ from the way any people attempt to identify themselves with the highest. The problem in this method is that the highest ceases to critique one's life style, and merely becomes a reflection of it.

6. In this corruption of Christianity, religion ceases to stand apart and critique culture. Religion becomes coopted by nationalism; national values, authority symbols and policies are interpreted as Christian values, authority symbols, and policies. Excellent articles on this subject can be found in *American Civil Religion* (New York: Harper & Row, 1974), ed. by Russell E. Richey and Donald G. Jones.

7. Howard Thurman, "Fascist Masquerade," Chapter 4 in *The Church and Organized Movements*, ed. by Randolph Crump Miller ("The Interseminary Series") (New York: Harper and Brothers, 1946), p. 94.

8. Thurman, *Luminous Darkness*, pp. 61-64.

9. In his book, *The Dark Center: A Process Theology of Blackness* (New York: Paulist Press, 1973), pp. 42-56, Eulalio R. Baltazar develops an insightful thesis which identifies Western color symbolism (and therefore racial attitudes) with certain Western philosophies (i.e., Calvin's concept of election, utilitarianism, social Darwinism, and pragmatism) which pro-

mote the idea that light is superior to dark. It is not difficult, therefore, to see how the white Christian might be accused of arrogance in his or her missionary role to blacks.

10. Howard Thurman, "Introduction," *Why I Believe There Is A God: Sixteen Essays by Negro Clergymen* (Chicago: Johnson Publishing Co., 1965), p. xi.

11. Howard Thurman, *Deep River and The Negro Spiritual Speaks of Life and Death,* originally separate books, but now in a single volume. *Deep River* was first published by Eucalyptus Press, 1945; and a revised edition by Harper and Brothers, 1955. *The Negro Spiritual Speaks of Life and Death* was first published by Harper and Brothers, 1947; the new reprint edition of both books (Richmond, IN. Friends United Press, 1975), p. 135.

12. *Ibid.*

13. Howard Thurman, *Luminous Darkness*, pp. 8, 106 and 107.

14. Thurman, *Disinherited*, p. 75.

15. Henry Nelson Wieman, *Methods of Private Religious Living* (New York: Macmillan Co., 1929), p. 140.

16. Thurman, *Luminous Darkness*, p. 24.

17. Howard Thurman, "Human Freedom and the Emancipation Proclamation," *Pulpit Digest*, December 1962, p. 14.

18. Thurman, *Luminous Darkness*, pp. 27-28.

19. *Ibid.*, pp. 26-27.

20. In his article "Fascist Masquerade" he says:It is to the utter condemnation of the Church that large groups of believers all over the United States have stood, and, at present, stand on the side of a theory of inequality among men that causes the Church to practice in its own body some of the most vicious forms of racial prejudice . . . The bitter truth is that the Church has permitted the various hate-inspired groups in our common life to establish squatter's rights in the minds of believers because there has been no adequate teaching of the meaning of the faith in terms of human dignity and human worth. (pp.97-98)

21. Thurman, *Disinherited*, p.98.

22. Howard Thurman, a sermon entitled "America in Search of a Soul," 20 January 1976.

23 Sydney E. Ahlstrom in his *A Religious History of the American People* notes this as a major theme in the making of the nation. (p. 7)

24. Howard Thurman, a sermon entitled "The American Dream," 6 June 1958. The aligning of political history with divine will sounds similar to the proponents of American civil religion. For Thurman, however, the birth of the nation represents a time of possibility, rather than a sanctioning and sanctification of the history and present policies of the country.

25. Thurman, *The Search for Common Ground*, pp. 87-88.

26. Thurman, "Fascist Masquerade," p. 87.

27. Thurman, "Mysticism and Social Change," p. 23.

28. *Ibid.*, p. 31.

29. Thurman, *Luminous Darkness*, pp. 89-90.

30. *Ibid.*, p. 101.

31. Howard Thurman, "Religion in a Time of Crisis," *The Garrett Tower*, Garrett Biblical Institute, Evanston, Illinois, August 1943, p. 3.

32. Howard Thurman, "The Christian Minister and the Desegregation Decision," *Pulpit Digest*, May 1957, pp. 13-19.

33. Thurman, *Luminous Darkness*, pp. 3-16.

34. *Ibid.*, pp. 26-27.

35. Thurman, *The Search for Common Ground*, p. 102.

36. *Ibid.*, p. 102.

37. Thurman, *Luminous Darkness*, p. 33.

38. *Ibid.*, pp. 42-44.

39. *Ibid.*, pp. 57-59; and *Disinherited*, p. 100.

40. Thurman, "Mysticism and Social Change," p. 33.

41. Howard Thurman, "The Will to Segregation," *Fellowship*, August 1943, p. 146.

42. Howard Thurman, "Peace Tactics and a Racial

Minority," *The World Tomorrow*, December 1928, pp. 505-507.

43. Thurman, *Disinherited*, pp. 89-109.

44. Thurman, *Disciplines*, pp. 104-127.

45. *Ibid.*, p. 113; and Thurman, *The Search for Common Ground*, p. 104.

46. James Weldon Johnson, *Negro Americans, What Now?* (New York: Viking Press: 1934), p. 81.

47. *Ibid.*, pp. 72 and 85.

48. Thurman, *Disciplines*, pp. 114-115.

49. Yates, *Howard Thurman*, pp. 104-109.

50. Thurman, *Deep Is the Hunger*, pp, 10-11.

51. Reinhold Niebuhr, *Moral Man and Immoral Society* (New York: Charles Scribners Sons, 1932), p. 252.

52. S.P. Fullwinder, *The Mind and Mood of Black America* (Homewood, IL: Dorsey Press, 1969, p. 239.

53. *Ibid.*, p. 239.

54. Lerone Bennett, Jr.,*What Manner of Man* (Chicago: Johnson Publishing Co., 1968), pp. 73-75 and further information on this sighting was shared in a letter (10 October 1977) from Mr. Bennett to the writer.

55. Hanes Walton, Jr., *The Political Philosophy of Martin Luther King, Jr.* (Conn.: Greenwood Publishing, 1971), pp. 28-30.

56. Howard Thurman, *With Head and Heart: The Autobiography of Howard Thurman* (New York: Harcourt Brace Javanovich, 1979), p. 144.

57. *Ibid.*, pp. 147-148.

58. *Ibid.*, p. 160.

59. Thurman, *Luminous Darkness*, p. 85.

60. Niebuhr, *Moral Man and Immoral Society*, pp. xxii-xxiii.

61. Smith interview with Thurman, 13 June 1977.

62. Thurman, "Mysticism and Social Change," p. 29.

63. Niebuhr, *Moral Man and Immoral Society*, pp. 249 and 273.

64. Reinhold Niebuhr, *An Interpretation of Christian Ethics* (New York: Harper & Brothers, 1935), p. 140.

65. Thurman, "Mysticism and Social Change," pp. 27-34; and Thurman, *Growing Edge*, pp. 77-84.

66. Thurman, *Disciplines*, p. 119.

67. *Ibid.*, p. 121. Paul Tillich's *Love, Power, and Justice: Ontological Analysis and Ethical Applications* (New York: Oxford University Press 1954) argues for an understanding of the distinct character and role of these concepts. To fully comprehend one, the others must also receive considerable attention.

68. Cross, *What is Christianity*, p. 182.

69. Niebuhr, *Interpretation of Christian Ethics*, p. 85.

70. Even Niebuhr concludes that nonviolence has an important spiritual role in social change; it sustains a moral factor which cannot be ignored. See *Moral Man and Immoral Society*, pp. 248-256.

71. Raymond L. Whitehead, *Love and Struggle in Mao's Thought* (Maryknoll, NY.: Orbis Books, 1977), p. 128.

72. Richard B. Gregg, *The Power of Nonviolence*, 2nd rev. ed. (New York: Schocken Books, 1966) pp. 15-42. Other convincing books on the ethical superiority and social change effectiveness of nonviolence are William Robert Miller's *Nonviolence: A Christian Interpretation* (New York: Association Press, 1964) and sociologist Pitirim A. Sorokins *The Ways and Power of Love* (Boston: Beacon Press, 1954).

73. Saul D. Alinsky, *Rules for Radicals: A Practical Primer for Realistic Radicals* (New York: Random House, 1971), p. 41.

74. Colin Morris, *Unyoung-Uncolored-Unpoor* (Nashville: Abingdon Press, 1969), p. 87.

75. Thurman, "The American Dream."

76. Yates, *Howard Thurman*, pp. 105-106.

77. Whitehead, *Mao's Thought*, p. xvii.

78. Alinsky, *Rules for Radicals*, p. 14.

79. James H. Cone, *Black Theology and Black Power* (New York: Seabury Press, 1969), p. 143.

80. Though liberation theologians and many social philosophers may speak to the necessity for the empowering of social mechanisms to effect change,

few of them discuss the details of economic and political strategies. Where does one begin to organize and apply the pressure? What suggested blueprints can be followed? These advocates of action are usually fast with theory and rationale, and slow in fleshing out and testing their ideas in particular contexts. This is not to denigrate their role, but to vindicate Thurman's position among them.

81. Thurman, *Disinherited* p. 62.

82. Smith interview with Thurman in November 1975 and on 28 June 1976.

Chapter V

1. Thurman, *Meditations of the Heart*, p. 15.

2. Comment was made by Howard Thurman during a seminar at the Howard Thurman Educational Trust, 23 January 1975.

3. Thurman, *Footprints of a Dream*, pp. 15-17.

4. *Ibid.*, pp. 19-20.

5. Smith interview with Thurman, 28 June 1976.

6. *Ibid.*

7. Thurman, *Footprints of a Dream*, p. 16.

8. Yates, *Howard Thurman*, p. 24.

9. *Ibid.*, p. 25.

10. *Ibid.*, pp. 26-27.

11. Howard Thurman, ed. An Introduction to *A Track to the Water's Edge: The Olive Schreiner Reader*, by Olive Schreiner (New York: Harper & Row, 1973), pp. xxvii-xxviii.

12. Thurman, *Footprints of a Dream*, p. 16.

13. Thurman, "Mysticism and Jesus."

14. Goodwin, "Racial Roots," p. 534.

15. Thurman, "Mysticism and Jesus."

16. Thurman, *Meditations of the Heart*, pp. 17-19, 27-28, 29-31.

17. Thurman, *Deep Is the Hunger*, pp. 169-170.

18. Thurman, *Inward Journey*, p. 131.

19. Seminar with Howard Thurman at the Howard Thurman Educational Trust, 29 January 1975.

20. Thurman, *Footprints of a Dream*, p. 9.

21. The terms "charisma" and "charismatic" are not used in the sense of describing: 1) one who has abilities from divine powers to speak in tongues, heal, or perform miracles; or 2) one who is part of the recent neo-pentecostal movement. The terms are applied to describe "a personal magic of leadership arousing special popular loyalty or enthusiasm. . ." (The definition is from *Webster's Seventh New Collegiate Dictionary,* 1972 ed.)

22. Frederick D. Harper, "Self-actualization and Three Black Protesters," *Contemporary Black Issues in Social Psychology* (A Collection of Major Articles Selected from *The Journal of Afro-American Issues,* 1972-1975): 57-73.

23. Abraham H. Maslow, *Motivation and Personality* (New York: Harper & Row, 1954), p. 150.

24. *Ibid,* pp. 153-174. All references to Maslow's categories are within these pages.

25. The use of Maslow's model is not meant to suggest that it is an infallible theory for categorizing Thurman's personality. Frank G. Goble, whose *The Third Force* is a critical study of Maslow's psychology, says Maslow's methodology for developing the self-actualization paradigm in some ways fails to meet strict standards of scientific investigation. It was impossible to repeat some of the situations which are examples for the model, and some personal data about subjects was not available. Goble concludes, however, that Maslow's theory has considerable value in explaining personality traits of people who make significant contributions to humanity. Among psychologists, Maslow's work is considered a major theory in describing the healthy personality. Recognizing the broad acceptance of Maslow's theory, and recognizing its language of actualization which makes it particularly applicable to the interests of Thurman, the paradigm is used as a tool which might provide some enlightenment for understanding Thurman's personality and its affect. See Frank G. Goble's *The Third Force: The Psychology of Abraham Maslow,* Foreword by Abraham Maslow (New York: Grossman Publishers, 1970), pp. 22-23;

and Sidney M. Jourard's *Personal Adjustment: An Approach Through the Study of Healthy Personality* (New York: Macmillan Co., 1958), pp. 7-8, 17, 18, and 161.

26. Goble, *Third Force*, p. 31.

27. Paul Chaffee, "The Spiritual Ground of Pastoral Theology: The Life and Thought of Howard Thurman," presented at a workshop for the 1977 Earl Lectures, Pacific School of Religion, February 1977, p. 5.

28. Barr interview with Thurman.

29. Marcus H. Boulware, *The Oratory of Negro Leaders: 1900-1968* (Westport, Conn.: Negro Universities Press, 1969), p. 73.

30. "Great Preachers," *Ebony*, July 1954, p. 26.

31. "Great Preachers," *Life*, 6 April 1953, p. 127.

32. Boulware, *Oratory of Negro Leaders*, p. 186.

33. Yates, *Howard Thurman*, p. 206.

34. James William McClendon, Jr., *Biography as Theology: How Life Stories Can Remake Today's Theology* (Nashville: Abingdon Press, 1974), pp. 37-38.

Chapter VI

1. Abraham J. Heschel, *The Prophets: Volume I* (New York: Harper & Row, 1962), p. 26.

2. Abraham J. Heschel, *The Prophets: Volume II* (New York: Harper & Row, 1962), p. 263.

3. Walter Brueggemann, *The Prophetic Imagination* (Philadelphia: Fortress Press, 1978), p. 111.

4. Reinhold Niebuhr, *Justice and Mercy*, ed. Ursula M. Niebuhr (New York: Harper & Row, 1974), p. v.

5. Benita Eisler, "Keeping the Faith," *The Nation*, 5-12 January 1980, p. 24.

6. Rosemary Radford Ruether, *Liberation Theology: Human Hope Confronts Christian History and American Power* (New York; Paulist Press, 1972), p. 12.

7. Martin Luther King, Jr., *Where Do We Go From Here: Chaos or Community?* (Boston: Beacon Press, 1967), pp. 100-101.

8. Jan Corbett, "Howard Thurman: A Theologian for Our Time," *The American Baptist*, December 1979, p. 10.

9. Before commenting on Thurman's remarks at a banquet of the National Committee of Black Churchmen, Cornish Rogers introduces him as the "spiritual mentor of most black churchmen over 35. . ." See Cornish Rogers, "NCBC: Streamlining for New Directions," *The Christian Century*, 25 October 1972, p. 1060.

10. Thurman *Luminous Darkness*, book jacket.

11. Vernon Jordan, Memorial Services tribute to Howard Thurman (a taped message), San Francisco, California, 16 April 1981.

12. Vincent Harding, "America in Search of a Soul," a lecture given at the Howard Thurman Convocation, Vanderbilt Divinity School, 27 October 1989. [This statement seemed so significant, that it is being included in this revised edition.]

13. Hans Massaquoi, "Ebony Interview with the Rev. Jesse Jackson," *Ebony*, June 1981, p. 155.

14. Jesse Jackson Memorial Services tribute to Howard Thurman, San Francisco, California, 16 April 1981.

15. Bennett, "Howard Thurman," p. 70.

16. Harold E. Quinley's *The Prophetic Clergy: Social Activism Among Protestant Ministers* (New York: John Wiley & Sons, 1974).

17. Watts, *Behold the Spirit*, p. 24.

18. *Ibid.*, p. xiii.

19. *Ibid.*, p. 61.

20. Rodney Stark and Charles Y. Glock, *American Piety: The Nature of Religious Commitment* (Berkeley: University of California Press, 1968), p. 216.

21. See Milton C. Sernett, *Black Religion and American Evangelicalism: White Protestants, Plantation Missions, and the Flowering of Negro Christianity, 1787-1865* (Metuchen, NJ.: Scarecrow Press, Inc., and The American Theological Library Association, 1975); and Monroe Fordham, *Major Themes in Northern Black Religious Thought, 1800-1860* (Hicksville, NY.: Exposition Press, 1975).

22. See Paul Tillich, *The Courage to Be* (New Haven: Yale University Press, 1952), p. 160.

23. See Cone's *Black Theology and Black Power*, p. 92; *God of the Oppressed*, pp. 31 and 249 n. 13; and *The Spirituals and the Blues: An Interpretation* (New York: Seabury Press, 1972), pp. 16-17, 50, 76, 84, and 96.

24. Cone, *God of the Oppressed*, p. 31.

25. Cone, *The Spirituals and the Blues*, p. 16.

26. Lerone Bennett, Jr., "The Crisis of the Black Spirit," *Ebony*, October 1977, p. 142.

27. Alex Poinsett, "PUSH for Excellence," *Ebony*, February 1977, p. 105.

28 The ever present urge to settle for homogeneous communities is evident in C. Peter Wagner's *Our Kind of People* (Atlanta: John Knox, 1979).

29 See Thurman, *The Search for Common Ground*.

30 Thurman, *Deep Is the Hunger*, p. 39.

31 Thurman, *The Search for Common Ground*, p. 103.

32 *Ibid.*, p. 104.

BIBLIOGRAPHY

THE WRITINGS OF HOWARD THURMAN

I. Books and Pamphlets

Thurman, Howard. *Apostles of Sensitiveness.* Boston:
American Unitarian Association, 1956

———. *The Centering Moment.* New York: Harper & Row,
1969. Richmond, IN.: Friends United Press, 1980.

———. *The Creative Encounter: An Interpretation
of Religion and the Social Witness.* New York: Harper
& Brothers, 1954. Richmond, IN.: Friends United
Press, 1972.

———. *Deep Is The Hunger.* New York: Harper & Brothers,
1951. Richmond, IN.: Friends United Press, 1973.

———. *Deep River: An Interpretation of Negro
Spirituals.* Mills College, CA.: Eucalyptus Press, 1975.

———. *Deep River and the Negro Spiritual Speaks
of Life and Death.* Single volume. Richmond, IN.:
Friends United Press, 1975.

———. *Disciplines of the Spirit.* New York: Harper & Row
1963. Richmond, IN.: Friends United Press, 1977.

———. *Footprints of A Dream: The Story of the
Church for the Fellowship of All Peoples.*
New York: Harper & Row, 1959.

———. *For the Inward Journey: The Writings of
Howard Thurman.* Selections by Ann
Spencer Thurman. New York: Harcourt, Brace
Javanovich, 1984. Richmond, IN.: Friends United
Press, 1991.

———. *The Greatest of These.* Mills College, CA.:
Eucalyptus Press, 1944.

———. *The Growing Edge.* New York: Harper & Row, 1956.
Richmond, IN.: Friends United Press, 1972.

———. *The Inward Journey.* New York: Harper & Row,
1961. Richmond, IN.: Friends United Press, 1971.

———. *Jesus and the Disinherited.* Nashville: Abindgon-
Cokesbury Press, 1949. Richmond, IN.:
Friends United Press, 1981.

———. *The Luminous Darkness: A Personal Interpretation*

247

of the Anatomy of Segregation and the
Ground of Hope. New York: Harper & Row, 1965.
Richmond, IN.: Friends United Press, 1989.

_____. *Meditations for Apostles of Sensitiveness*.
Mills College, CA: Eucalyptus Press, 1947.

_____. *The Mood of Christmas*. New York: Harper & Row,
1973. Richmond, IN.: Friends United Press, 1985.

_____. *Mysticism and the Experience of Love*.
Wallingford, PA.: Pendle Hill Pamphlet 115, 1961.

_____. *The Negro Spiritual Speaks of Life and Death*.
New York: Harper & Brothers, 1947.

_____. *The Search for Common Ground: An Inquiry into
the Basis of Man's Experience of Community*. New
York: Harper & Row, 1971. Richmond, IN.: Friends
United Press, 1986.

_____. *Temptations of Jesus: Five Sermons*. San Francisco:
Lawton Kennedy, Printer, 1962. Richmond, IN.:
Friends United Press, 1978.

_____. *With Head and Heart: The Autobiography of Howard
Thurman*. New York: Harcourt Brace Jovanovich,
1979.

_____. ed. *The First Footprints: The Dawn of the Idea of the
Church for the Fellowship of All Peoples: Letters
Between Alfred Fisk and Howard Thurman 1943-
1944*. San Francisco: Lawton and Alfred Kennedy,
1975.

_____. Editor and Introduction to *A Track to the Water's
Edge: The Olive Schreiner Reader*, by Olive Schreiner.
New York: Harper & Row, 1973.

II. Contributions to Books

Thurman, Howard. "And When Thou Prayest."
Sermons From An Ecumenical Pulpit.
Chapter 9. Edited by Max F. Daskam.
Boston: Starr King Press, 1956, pp. 86-90.

_____.Thurman, Howard. "Exposition to the Book of
Habakkuk." *The Interpreter's Bible*, Vol. 6.
Edited by George A. Buttrick et al.
Nashville: Abingdon Press, 1956, pp. 979-1002.

_____. "Exposition to the Book of Zephaniah."
The Interpreter's Bible, Vol. 6. Edited by

George A. Buttrick et al. Nashville:
Abingdon Press, 1956, pp. 1013-1034.

_____. "Fascist Masquerade." *The Church and
Organized Movements.* Chapter 4. Edited
by Randolph Crump Miller ("The Interseminary
Series"). New York: Harper & Brothers, 1946,
pp. 82-100.

_____. "Finding God." *Religion on the Campus.* Edited by
Francis P. Miller. New York: Association Press, 1927,
pp. 48-52.

_____. "God and the Race Question." *Together.* Chapter 12.
Compiled by Glenn Clark. Nashville: Abingdon-
Cokesbury Press, 1946, pp. 118-120.

_____. "Good News for the Underprivileged." *The Negro
Caravan.* Edited by Sterling A. Brown. New York:
The Citadel Press, 1940, pp. 685-692; reprinted from
the 1935 article in *Religion in Life.*

_____. "The Greatest of These." *The Preaching Pastor.*
Edited by Charles F. Kemp. St. Louis: Bethany Press,
1966, pp. 123-127. Reprinted from Thurman's book
The Growing Edge, pp. 24-28.

_____. "Introduction." *Why I Believe There Is A God: Sixteen
Essays by Negro Clergymen.* Chicago: Johnson
Publishing Co., Inc., 1965, pp. v-xi.

_____. "Judgment and Hope in the Christian Message." *The
Christian Way in Race Relations.* Chapter 12. Edited
by William Stuart Nelson. New York: Harper &
Brothers, 1948, pp. 229-235.

_____. "From 'The Luminous Darkness'." *Viewpoints from
Black America.* Edited by Gladys J. Curry.
Englewood Cliffs, NJ.: Prentice-Hall Inc., 1970, pp.
207-212. Reprinted from Thurman's book *The
Luminous Darkness,* pp. 102-109.

_____. "The Meaning of Purpose in Religious Experience."
Religion Ponders Science. Chapter 15. Edited by
Edwin P. Booth. New York: Appleton-Century, 1964,
pp. 266-278.

_____. "The Meaning of Spirituals." *The Negro In Music and
Art.* Edited by Lindsey Patterson. New York:
Publishers Co., 1967.

_____. "Mysticism and Ethics." *The Journal of Religious Thought.* Summer Supplement 1970, pp. 23-30.

_____. "Mysticism and Social Change." *Eden Theological Seminary Bulletin,* Spring 1939, pp. 3-34.

_____. "The Religion of Jesus and the Disinherited." *In Defense of Democracy.* Edited by T. H. Johnson. N.P., n.d., pp. 125-135.

III. Single Sermons, Addresses, and Articles

Thurman, Howard. "Christ's Message to the Disinherited." *Ebony,* Centennial Issue, September 1963, pp. 58-62.

_____. "The Christian Minister and the Desegregation Decision." *Pulpit Digest,* May 1957, pp. 13-19.

_____. "The Church and the Administrator." *California Elementary School Administrators Association Yearbook,* 1953, pp. 162-164.

_____. "Deep River." *Pulpit Digest,* January 1956, pp. 81-97.

_____. "The Discipline of Reconciliation." *Journal of Religion and Health,* October 1963, pp. 7-26. Reprinted from his book *Disciplines of the Spirit,* pp. 104-127.

_____. "The Fellowship Church of All Peoples." *Common Ground,* Spring Issue 1945, pp. 29-31.

_____. "For A Time of Sorrow." *The Christian Century,* 26 July 1953, p. 867.

_____. "Good News for the Underprivileged." *Religion in Life,* Summer Issue 1935, pp. 403-409. Reprinted in *The Negro Caravan.* Edited by Sterling A. Brown. New York: The Citadel Press, 1940, pp. 685-692.

_____. "The Great Incarnate Words." *Motive* Magazine, January 1944, p. 24.

_____. "The Ground of Hope." *The Saturday Evening Post,* January/February 1980, pp. 42, 44, 47, and 114.

_____. "Human Freedom and the Emancipation Proclamation." *Pulpit Digest,* December 1962, pp. 13-16, 66.

_____. "I Will Light Three Candles." *Parents* Magazine, December 1949, p. 26.

_____. "Interracial Church in San Francisco." *Social Action,* 15 February 1945, pp. 27-28.

_____. "Keep Awake!" *The Christian Century Pulpit,* June

1937, pp. 125-127.

———. "The New Heaven and the New Earth." *The Journal of Negro Education* XXVIII (1958): 115-119.

———. "Peace Tactics and a Racial Minority." *The World Tomorrow*, December 1928, pp. 505-507.

———. "Putting Yourself in Another's Place." *Childhood Education*, February 1962, pp.259-260.

———. "Putting Yourself in Another's Place." *Child Guidance in Christian Living* XXII (February 1963): 9. Reprint of the 1962 article in *Childhood Education*.

———. "The Quest for Stability." *The Woman's Press*, April 1949.

———. "Religion in a Time of Crisis." *The Garrett Tower*. Garrett Biblical Institute. Evanston, IL.: n.p., August 1943.

———. "Religious Ideas in Negro Spirituals." *Christendom*, August 1939, pp. 515-528.

———. "The Search for Common Ground." *Perspective:* A Journal of Pittsburgh Theological Seminary XIII (Spring 1972): 127-137.

———. "The Search for God in Religion." *The Laymen's Movement Review*, November-December 1962.

———. "What Can We Believe In?" *The Journal of Religion and Health* 12 (April 1973): 111-119.

———. "What Shall I Do With My Life?" *The Christian Century Pulpit*, September 1939, pp. 210-211.

IV. Book Reviews

Thurman, Howard. Review of J. Deotis Roberts's *Liberation and Reconciliation: A Black Theology.* In *Religious Education*, November-December 1971, pp. 464-466.

———. Review of William Douglass Chamberlain's *The Manner of Prayer.* In *The Journal of Religious Thought* I (1943-1944): 179.

———. Review of Douglas V. Steere's *On Beginning from Within.* In *The Journal of Religion*, October 1944, pp. 284-285.

———. Review of Richard I. McKinney's *Religion in Higher Education Among Negroes.* In *Religion in Life*, Autumn Number 1946, pp. 619-620.

V. Taped Sermons, Lectures, Meditations, Interviews, and Discussions: over 800 tapes of these oral presentations are in the library of the Howard Thurman Educational Trust, 2018 Stockton, San Francisco, CA. The Trust has catalogs of tapes which are available to the public.

CPSIA information can be obtained
at www.ICGtesting.com
Printed in the USA
FFOW05n0209050917